DISCARDED

SHAKESPEARE'S ENGLAND

The time of William Shakespeare (1564–1616) has been christened England's Golden Age. This new title in the PUTNAM PICTORIAL SOURCES SERIES contains hundreds of contemporary illustrations carefully chosen to re-create this great period. It studies the work of contemporary painters and miniaturists; composers for voices, lute, and keyboard such as Thomas Tallis and Orlando Gibbons; writers and philosophers, including Francis Bacon and Thomas Hobbes; and the great Elizabethan and Jacobean poets like young John Milton. It examines how far, in Shakespeare's England, the Crown, Church and Parliament together dominated national affairs and how ordinary people were caught up in the great religious and political issues of the day. We see how some of them were martyred for their beliefs or, like the Pilgrim Fathers, sought a purer life in the New World or, like Robert Catesby and Guido Fawkes, plotted to overthrow the régime. Dr. Fox illustrates the quality of life for townspeople and country folk, constantly menaced by bubonic plague, lawlessness, superstition, and economic depression, but eagerly pursuing the pleasures of life afforded by the great feast days, markets and fairs, and such pastimes as an arduous subsistence living would permit. In sharp contrast, he discusses the life of the great men—lords, bishops, and merchants. The foundation of the East India Company in 1600 was a landmark of this age of expansion. Merchants, astronomers, scientists, and explorers combined to extend the horizons of the known world and to make possible the early colonization of North America. As Dr. Fox shows, William Shakespeare himself not only witnessed, but helped create that revitalization of English life and thought that marked the dawn of a more modern and civilized age.

Fama:

PRÆTOR LONDINENSIS

A PUTNAM PICTORIAL SOURCES BOOK

SHAKESPEARE'S ENGLAND

LEVI FOX

G. P. PUTNAM'S SONS . NEW YORK

The Putnam Pictorial Sources Series

Voyages of Discovery   G. R. CRONE AND A. KENDALL
The French Revolution   DOUGLAS JOHNSON
The Medieval Establishment   GEOFFREY HINDLEY
The American Revolution   ROGER PARKINSON
Medieval Warfare   GEOFFREY HINDLEY
The American Civil War   KEITH ELLIS
Twentieth Century China   JOHN ROBOTTOM
The Russian Revolution   LIONEL KOCHAN
The Dawn of Man   VINCENT MEGAW AND RHYS JONES

Frontispiece: Top "Elizabeth and Fame", an
imaginary scene from a book by William Teshe.
Bottom officials of London in Elizabeth I's
funeral procession.

Copyright © 1972 by Wayland (Publishers) Ltd
This edition first published in 1972 by G. P. Putnam's Sons,
200 Madison Avenue, New York, N.Y. 10016
All rights reserved. This book, or parts thereof, must not be
reproduced in any form without permission
Published simultaneously in Canada by
Longmans Canada Limited, Toronto.
Library of Congress Catalog Card Number: 72–185488.
Printed in England.

CONTENTS

CHAPTER ONE

ENGLAND'S GOLDEN AGE

INTRODUCTION

The years which cover the life of William Shakespeare (1564–1616) have been described as "the most glorious, and in some ways the most significant, period of English history." The fascination is understandable. Victorian writers found the Age of Elizabeth picturesque, giving full scope for their sentimental respect and imaginative interpretations. Stripped of its glamour, to us it was a period of transition from Tudor absolutism to parliamentary government; an age of contrasts and contradictions, of religious and political conflict, of rural change, of adventure and discovery; a time of re-assessment when new ideas and practices gave fresh impetus and enrichment to national life; a period of great achievement in literature, the arts, the theatre, music and natural science; days when, although transport and communications were slow, spirits and national pride were running high; the era which produced Sir Francis Drake and Philip Sidney, Sir Francis Bacon and Sir Walter Raleigh, Edmund Spenser and Shakespeare, not to mention Queen Elizabeth herself.

Thanks to the abundant source material that has survived, and to the painstaking research of scholars in recent years, the period is not "something dead and apart from us," but as Dr. Rowse, the Elizabethan historian, has demonstrated, it is "alive and all around us and within us." Numerous buildings together with furnishings and personal items belonging to the period have survived intact. In addition the public records, private collections, the writings of contemporaries and pictorial material of many kinds make possible a detailed knowledge of Shakespeare's England. Moreover, though men and women may be different now in the things they do—the physical framework of life has inevitably changed—in themselves, that is in what they are, they are essentially the same.

Shakespeare could not have chosen a more exciting or inspiring time to be born. Although the Wars of the Roses were long over and the Tudor monarchy firmly established, much of Europe during Shakespeare's lifetime was ravaged by war, religious conflict, cruelty and political self-seeking. The Civil War and Puritan Revolution still lay far ahead, but the traditional concept of monarchy was already being questioned by some, and potents of the coming clash between sovereign and Parliament showed themselves from time to time, particularly after James I's accession.

The London Shakespeare came to know was a busy, prosperous city notable for its palaces, fine houses and trading quarters, the seat of government, the law and the Court, with its beloved River Thames affording unrivalled facilities for shipping and commerce. It had its narrow squalid streets, but there were fields and open spaces too, and across the bridge on the south bank of the river lay the area where recreation, including the theatre, could take place outside the control of the City.

The people loved the Queen and she firmly held them in her affections; they shared with her pride in the exploits of their seamen who had sailed strange seas, carrying the English flag into parts hitherto unknown and returning with treasure and tales of adventure and glory.

This was also a time of economic and social change: the middle class was emerging, capitalism was trying its wings, and every week brought new ventures, speculations and discoveries. Life in the capital was vigorous if hazardous, with no lack of opportunity for the industrious or idle. There were extremes of wealth and poverty but a new civic conscience about the needs of the poor was growing. Education was spreading through newly established schools. The writing and performance of plays met with a steady demand and in spite of Puritan disapproval attracted royal patronage. Foreign visitors to the capital could frequently be seen and the City was closely in touch with its home and overseas markets. There were writers, even as today, expounding their views on religious and social problems, holding forth against tobacco, alcohol, the conduct of young people and the dress and primping of women. Outdoor games and recreation, with the favourite pastimes of bull and bear baiting took care of the scanty leisure time of the workers; gambling, drunkedness and brothels were not unknown. Beggars and cutpurses presented a particular problem, as did the traffic and crowds described by one of Shakespeare's contemporaries, the playwright Thomas Dekker: "In every street, carts and coaches make such a thundering as if the world ran upon wheels. At every corner, men, women, and children meet in such shoals that posts are set up . . . to strengthen the houses, lest with jostling one another they should shoulder them down. Besides, hammers are beating in one place, tubs hooping in another, pots clashing in a third, water tankards running at a tilt in a fourth, Here are porters sweating under burdens, their merchant's men bearing bags of money. Chapmen (as if they were at leapfrog) skip out of one shop into another. Tradesmen . . . are busy at legs and never stand still."

Thus, like a cluster of jewels, the London of Shakespeare's time—itself a reflection of the country at large—had innumerable facets. The central gem was the Queen herself, surrounded by the ceremonial of a spectacular court adorned by ministers, gentlemen and ladies, the magnificence of whose attire evoked comment from all who saw them. Whatever the assessment of her character may be, there can be no doubt that she had a genius for kingship which enabled her to identify herself with the needs and feelings of the nation as none of her predecessors had ever done. To her people she became a symbol of their hatred of Spanish aggression and of their newly-found national pride.

In one of his earliest plays, *A Midsummer Night's Dream*, Shakespeare offered a touching tribute to "a fair vestal throned by the west," whom Cupid assailed in vain:

But I see young Cupid's fiery shaft
Quench'd in the chaste beams of the wat'ry moon
And the imperial votaress passed on,
In maiden meditation, fancy-free!

Again, looking back on the memory of the Queen, Shakespeare recalls her greatness in *King Henry VIII* in the form of a prophecy, spoken at her christening by Archbishop Cranmer:

This royal infant—heaven still move about her!—
Though now in her cradle, yet now promises
Upon this land a thousand thousand blessings,
Which time shall bring a ripeness: she shall be—
But few now living can behold that goodness—
A pattern to all princes living with her,
And all that shall succeed . . .
In her days every man shall eat in safety
Under his own vine what he plants, and sing
The merry songs of peace to all his neighbours.
God shall be truly known; and those about her
From her shall read the perfect ways of honour,
And by those claim their greatness, not by blood.

Beloved and admired by her contemporaries Queen Elizabeth—like the age in which she lived—was in many respects an enigma. Possessed of all the feminine qualities and foibles she displayed all the characteristics and courage of a man. At once gentle yet imperious, susceptible to flattery yet unbelievably determined, she possessed a natural statecraft which enabled her to cope with all the problems of the national and international scene, thus conferring benefit, prestige and prosperity on the subjects she loved. At times she gave the impression that she would entertain the thought of marriage in deference to public opinion, but she manoeuvred with such tact and cunning so as to be able to keep herself a maiden Queen.

After Elizabeth's death in 1603, Thomas Dekker asserted that "Both in her life and death she was appointed to be the mirror of her time." Without Elizabeth there would certainly have been no Elizabethan age. In elaboration of this assertion the eulogy of Nicholas Breton, preserved in a manuscript in the British Museum, is all embracing: "During her life, what peace in her country! what plenty in her land! what triumphs in her court! what learning in her schools! what trades in her cities! what wealth in her kingdom! what wisdom in her counsel and what grace in her government! Who durst to annoy her but the enemies of God's word, who felt the hand of His wrath for seeking the hurt of His anointed? Whom held she her friends but the favourers of God's truth, and to whom was she an enemy but to the enemies of the same? What monarch ever sent to her whose ambassador did not admire her, and what prince did ever hear of her who did not worthily honour her? Was she not mistress of the narrow seas and feared even in the ocean? Did not the heathen know her power and Christians sue for her favour? O let me speak of her majesty but with admiration whom God had blessed with so much perfection! Was not the soldier rewarded, the scholar cherished, the lawyer advanced, the merchant enriched and the tradesman maintained? Yea, had not the rich their pleasure and the poor their relief, the stranger pity and the subject peace—and all under the hand of God, in the eye of her grace and care of her government—and can all this be forgotten? Did not her trumpets sound rather passa measures than points of war, and her drums rather beat dances than warlike marches, and her horses not rather neigh in the pride of their furniture than in fury against the enemy? Was not music in her best key in her court, and what art was excellent in her kingdom that had not grace in her favour? What state in more majesty, what court in more state, what counsel in more honour, and what honour in more grace?"

To complete this introduction to the descriptions and illustrations of aspects of Shakespeare's England which follow another contemporary impression of England and the English during Elizabeth's reign—the view of a foreigner, Paul Hentzner who visited England in 1598—may be allowed to speak for itself: "The English are grave like the Germans, lovers of shew; followed wherever they go by whole troops of servants, who wear their masters' arms in silver fastened to their left arms, and are not undeservedly ridiculed for wearing tails hanging down their backs. They excel in dancing and music, for they are active and lively, though of a thicker make than the French; they cut their hair close on the middle of the head, letting it grow on either side; they are good sailors, and better pirates, cunning, treacherous, and thievish; above 300 are said to be hanged annually at London. Beheading with them is less infamous than hanging. They give the wall as the place of honour. Hawking is the common sport of the gentry. They are more polite in eating than the French, consuming less bread, but more meat, which they roast in perfection. They put a great deal of sugar in their drink. Their beds are covered with tapestry, even those of farmers. They are often molested with the scurvy, said to have first crept into England with the Norman conquest. Their houses are commonly of two stories, except in London, where they are of three and four, though but seldom of four; they are built of wood; those of the richer sort with bricks; their roofs are low, and where the owner has money, covered with lead. They are powerful in the field, successful against their enemies, impatient of anything like slavery; vastly fond of great noises that fill the ear, such as the firing of cannon, drums, and the ringing of bells, so that in London it is common for a number of them, that have got a glass in their heads, to go up into some belfry, and ring the bells for hours together, for the sake of exercise. If they see a foreigner, very well made or particularly handsome, they will say, 'It is a pity he is not an Englishman.'"

William Shakespeare (1) was born in Stratford-upon-Avon in 1564 in the house preserved as his Birthplace in Henley Street. On both sides his parents came of farming stock. His father, John Shakespeare, was a glover and wool dealer by trade, who played an active part in town affairs and in fact held the office of Bailiff. The Birthplace, as represented in an early drawing first published in 1769, was a big half-timbered building and by the standards of the time was a comfortable, middle-class home (2, 3). Little is known about William's boyhood, but he was almost certainly educated at the local grammar school. When just over 18 he married Anne Hathaway of Shottery and shortly afterwards left Stratford, according to tradition to avoid prosecution for a poaching offence. From 1592 onwards he can be traced in London first as an actor and then as a reviser and writer of plays.

1

2

3

The quality and popularity of his work soon excited the admiration and envy of his contemporaries, and his first poem, *Venus and Adonis* (1593), met with a warm reception. Next year came *The Rape of Lucrece* and from this time onward the production of Shakespeare's plays can be traced and dated by documentary evidence. Research has also established Shakespeare's association with companies of players, especially the Chamberlain's Men, and his partnership in various theatrical ventures. Some of his plays were published in separate form during his lifetime (4), but it was not until 1623, seven years after his death, that the first complete edition of his works—the First Folio (first edition)—containing his engraved portrait and Ben Jonson's eulogy appeared (5). By this time Shakespeare's monument in Stratford church had also been erected (page 41).

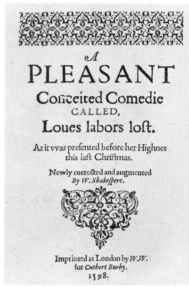

A PLEASANT

Conceited Comedie

CALLED,

Loues labors loft.

As it vvas prefented before her Highnes this laft Chriftmas.

Newly corrected and augmented By W. Shakefpere.

Imprinted at London by W.W. for Cutbert Burby. 1598.

4

5

To the Reader.

This *Figure*, that thou here feeft put,
It was for gentle *Shakefpeare* cut;
Wherein the *Grauer* had a ftrife
With *Nature*, to out-doe the *Life*:
O, could he but haue drawn his *Wit*
As well in *Braffe*, as he has hit
His *Face*; the *Print* would then furpaffe
All, that was euer writ in *Braffe*.
But fince he cannot, *Reader*, look
Not on his *Picture*, but his *Book*.

B. F.

12 Christopher Marlowe, son of a Canterbury shoemaker, was born the same year as Shakespeare (6). Unlike him, he had a university education at Corpus Christi College, Cambridge. His first play *Tamburlaine*, written in 1587, established his reputation as a master of blank verse; his tragedies which followed, especially *Doctor Faustus* (7) (produced in 1588 but not published till 1604), *The Jew of Malta* and *Edward II* placed him among the leading dramatists of the day. Without doubt Marlowe influenced Shakespeare and an examination of the plays *Titus Andronicus* and *Henry VI* has produced evidence that he may have written parts of them. He was killed in a tavern quarrel in 1593. Ben Jonson (1572–1637), after being educated at Westminster School in London, had helped in the business of his stepfather, a bricklayer and had seen military service in the Netherlands (8). He began his career as an

6

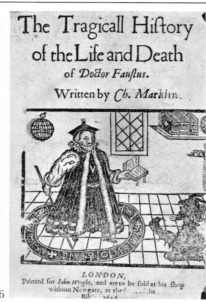

The Tragicall History of the Life and Death of *Doctor Faustus*.

Written by *Ch. Marklin*.

LONDON,
Printed for *John Wright*, and are to be sold at his shop without Newgate, at the ...of the Bible 1616.

7

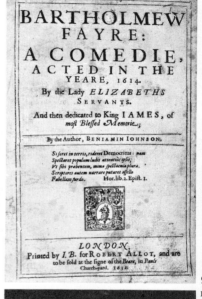

BARTHOLMEW FAYRE:
A COMEDIE,
ACTED IN THE
YEARE, 1614.
By the Lady *ELIZABETHS*
SERVANTS.

And then dedicated to King *IAMES*, of
most Blessed Memorie.

By the Author, *BENIAMIN IOHNSON*.

Si foret in terris, rideret Democritus: nam
Spectaret populum ludis attentius ipsis,
Vt sibi præbentem, mimo spectacula plura.
Scriptores autem narrare putaret asello
Fabellam surdo. Hor. lib. 2. Epist. 1.

LONDON,
Printed by *I.B.* for *ROBERT ALLOT*, and are
to be sold at the signe of the Beare, in Pauls
Church-yard. 1631.

9

1

8

10

actor and playwright in 1597 as a member of Henslowe's company and became a close friend and admirer of Shakespeare. His first important comedy, *Every Man in His Humour*, was first performed at the Curtain Theatre in 1598, with Shakespeare in the cast as a member of the Lord Chamberlain's Company. Jonson's output of dramatic writings was great, and he became famous as a producer of court masques. Jonson's comedy, *Bartholomew Fayre*, produced in 1614 and dedicated to James I, contains important references to the Theatre, to actors and to Shakespeare (9). Jonson had a wide circle of friends which included Francis Beaumont (10) and John Fletcher (11), whose plays were especially associated with the Blackfriars Theatre (12).

Mystery and miracle plays were staged on movable stages or as pageants outdoors (13). Performances took place in nearly a hundred towns and villages between 1300 and 1600 (page 42). Before London had any public theatres, plays were performed on makeshift stages in the courtyards of inns, in noblemen's houses, or in the home of the lawyers—the Inns of Court. The first two permanent playhouses were built in 1576, soon followed by the Swan Theatre (14). The best-known Eliza-

bethan playhouse was the Globe, built in 1598 by a partnership of actors, including Shakespeare (15). The Globe was the exclusive home of Shakespeare's company for the next ten years and it was during this period that his greatest plays were produced. When Shakespeare started his career as an actor–writer, theatrical entertainment was frowned upon by the Puritan Corporation of the City of London. Equally, acting was regarded as a vagabond profession and actors found it advisable

13

14

17

to obtain a patron. The best-known company was the Chamberlain's Men, originally formed under the patronage of Lord Chamberlain Hunsdon (16), and later styled the King's Men under King James I. Shakespeare himself belonged to it, and wrote for its productions. Other well-known members were William Kempe, the celebrated dancer who danced from London to Norwich, an event that he described in his *Kemps morris to Norwiche* (17); Richard Burbage, the younger son of James Burbage of the Theatre (18); Edward Alleyn, who played Marlowe's tragic heroes (19), and John Lowin (20) who played Falstaff, and as Henry VIII "had his instructions from Mr. Shakespear himself." Music was important in Shakespeare's plays. James I's reign (1603–24) saw the rise of the costly Court masque, notable for its high literacy, spectacular and musical qualities. The masque became very popular under Ben Jonson and the brilliant scenic designer, Inigo Jones.

18   20

16

19

21

Ability to sing or play was regarded as part of a person's education (22). There was great interest in all forms of music-making: playing instruments in consort, such as the viols (page 43); singing in vocal consort—the Elizabethans excelled in madrigals—or solo, often accompanied by lute, viol, recorder, virginal or harpsichord. Queen Elizabeth had her own virginal (23). In John Dowland, England had not only the greatest lutenist of the day but a composer of exquisite songs. Several collec-

tions of songs and keyboard pieces were published, for example by Dr. John Bull, the Queen's organist (24), and *Parthenia* (25), the first music printed for the virginals in 1611. The Royal Courts retained professional musicians, with trumpets and drums for state occasions and bands for banquets and balls. By the 1550s musical progress in England had fallen behind Italy and the Netherlands. The Wars of the Roses had lessened noble patronage, and the dissolution of the monasteries and

22
24

23

the chantries had almost killed Church music. Most English composers were compromised in adhering to the Roman communion. Then William Byrd (26), who joined Thomas Tallis as organist of the Chapel Royal in 1569, composed both for the Roman and the Anglican liturgies. The period produced some fine anthems and Anglican services as well as the Latin music of Byrd, Tallis, Philips and White. Falstaff's remark—"I would I were a weaver, I could sing psalms or anything"—reflects the popularity of English psalmody at this period. The re-establishment of the cathedral and collegiate foundations, such as that of St. George's, Windsor (27), helped English Church music. Secular music grew more popular and monopolies were granted to composers. In 1575, Byrd and Tallis were authorized to publish music and sell music-paper for twenty-one years.

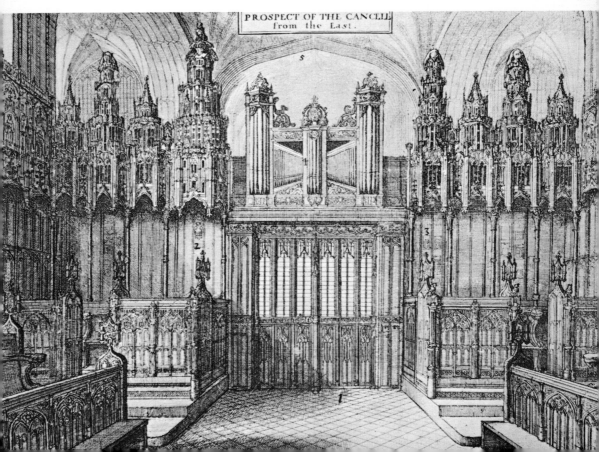

PROSPECT OF THE CANCLLE
from the East.

18 Despite Puritan hostility, painting flourished under Elizabeth. The portrait painter, or "picture-maker," found plenty of customers with long galleries to adorn. The Elizabethan artist gave most prominence to sumptuous clothing, armour, coats of arms, ceremonial robes and insignia of office (28). The most delicate and appealing of Elizabethan art forms was miniature painting, whose two greatest exponents were Nicholas Hilliard (29), and his pupil and rival Isaac Oliver. Hilliard,

who became portrait painter to the Queen, worked to catch the "lovely graces," "wittye smilings" and "stolne glances" which bring his miniatures so strikingly to life for us today. Hilliard liked to put extra elements into his miniatures, such as the love-sick young man amongst the soft petals and sharp thorns of the rose (30). The first Elizabethan age saw a considerable output of printed books reflecting at once an amazing thirst for knowledge and a desire to spread learning—books on history,

29

28

3

law, the classics, travel, falconry (31), natural history, theology and dictionaries. Shakespeare himself used the well-known English histories of his time written by Hall and Holinshed as the source of his history plays, while North's English translation of *Plutarch's Lives* (1603) provided the basis of his Roman plays. Queen Elizabeth herself was an accomplished linguist, and James I was a learned writer. It was the age of the enlightened amateur, as witnessed, for example, by Sir

Walter Raleigh's *History of the World*, published in 1614 (32). Among scholarly writers, George Chapman is particularly remembered for his rhyming Homer (33). His contemporary, Michael Drayton, completed his *Poly-Olbion* in 1622, a poem describing the natural curiosities of the English countryside, and carrying forward the work done in the previous century by John Leland and William Camden in his *Britannia* (1586).

32

33

The writing of lyric poetry, especially the sonnet, became very fashionable in England under Sir Thomas Wyatt (34), and Sir Philip Sidney (35). Sidney's *Stella* sonnets of 1591 inspired the writing of several sonnet sequences during the next few years, the finest being Shakespeare's. Most, if not all, of these had been written by 1598, when Meres refers to "his sugred Sonnets among his private friends." Sidney's *Arcadia* (1590) is a landmark because it is a prose romance, and forerunner of the novel (36). Together with Edmund Spenser, Fulke Greville, Gabriel Harvey, Edward Dyer and others, Sidney belonged to the Areopagus club, which advocated the introduction of classical metres into English verse. Preeminent among them was Edmund Spenser, famous for *The Shepherds' Calendar* (1579) (37), and *The Faerie Queene*. Shakespeare's England also produced some remarkable thinkers and

34

35

36

37

personalities. Thomas Campion, who died in 1619, was a physician. He also wrote masques for the Court, a treatise on music, lyrics, and songs on the death of Prince Henry. His views on English verse were expressed in his *The Art of English Poesie* (1602) in which he condemned "the vulgar and artificial custom of riming" (38). Few writers made money from their books. Some, like Lord Chancellor Bacon— "the wisest, brightest, meanest of mankind"—

combined a busy public life with a vast output of philosophical, literary and legal works (39). John Donne, the son of a London ironmonger, was another typical product of the times. His satires, elegies and sermons made a great impact and Ben Jonson rated him as "the first poet in some things." Mention should also be made of the philosopher Thomas Hobbes (40).

38

BSERVATIONS
in the Art of English
Poesie.

By *Thomas Campion.*

Vherein it is demonstra-
ely prooued, and by example
nfirmed, that the English toong
vill receiue eight seuerall kinds of num-
bers, proper to it selfe, which are all
in this booke set forth, and were
neuer before this time by any
man attempted.

rinted at London by RICHARD FIELD
for *Andrew Wise.* 1602.

39

40

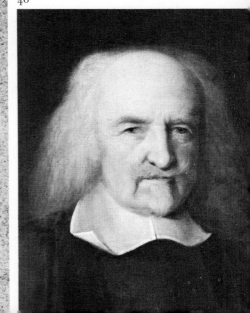

CHAPTER TWO
STATECRAFT

IN THEIR SCOPE and excellence the cultural achievements of the Elizabethan age, as illustrated in the previous chapter, represented an unparalleled enrichment of English national life. At a time when England was fighting for life against the Jesuits and the Spaniards, when Drake was sailing round the world and Gilbert and Raleigh were dreaming of the first English colonies, a new spirit of national confidence and independence expressed itself in a blossoming of the arts, and supremely in the dramatic writings of William Shakespeare. Yet, as has been suggested, the roots of the drama, music and literature of the period went deep into the previous centuries. The age of Elizabeth was essentially one of transition from the rigid outlook and ideas of the Middle Ages to the more enquiring, outward-looking spirit of the Renaissance, and the age of humanism that followed.

Shakespeare himself reflects both the old and the new ideas. He shows the medieval reverence for the anointed sovereign as a being set apart to rule; at the same time he echoes the growing idea that monarchs were fallible human beings. In *Hamlet*, for example, he deliberately depicts the royal family as frail human beings. Claudius, who has murdered the true king and usurped the throne, tries to console himself with the words:

> There's such divinity doth hedge a king,
> That treason can but peep to what it would,
> Acts little of his will   (IV, 5).

Claudius thus seeks comfort from the idea of kingship which had been common in the Middle Ages, and counts on the fact that people would respect him too much as king to harm him in revenge. Yet in order to become king, Claudius had killed the rightful king and was therefore a usurper. Legitimacy had been overthrown, with dire results.

Kingship and loyalty were themes frequently used by Shakespeare. As a supporter of kingship he often voiced the orthodox views of the paramount need for authority and the wickedness of rebellion. Hence the extreme reluctance of the Scottish nobles to make war even upon Macbeth. Macbeth—like Richard III— had to be painted as a tyrant and hateful monster to justify such resistance.

In Shakespeare's lifetime the whole concept of monarchy was undergoing radical change. Under the medieval system, everything had its fixed place in the world, indeed in the universe. If things got out of place, or out of control, then the whole balance and functioning of the universe, so it was thought, could be upset too. The monarch had a vital role to play in his ordered arrangement of life. For much of the sixteenth century the Tudor monarchs were able to rely on the ready acceptance of this idea by most of their subjects. The fixed order of things is referred to repeatedly by Shakespeare. The whole of the action of *King Lear*, for instance, is set on foot precisely because the king abdicates. The natural order of things is therefore overturned, and tragedy

22

follows. Yet while disaster is presented in *King Lear* as leading to every kind of evil, the abuse of authority is shown as an evil in itself and one which corrupts the whole fabric of the commonwealth:

> *There thou mightest behold the great image of authority:*
> *a dog's obeyed in office . . .*
> > *Plate sin with gold,*
> *And the strong lance of justice hurtless breaks;*
> *Arm it in rags, a pigmy's sword doth pierce it*　(IV, 6).

Shakespeare's support for the principle of monarchy was not uncritical. It is also clear that some of his contemporaries, such as Francis Bacon in his essay *Of Empire*, were also beginning to question the medieval concept.

Queen Elizabeth's great achievement was to behave as if she had God-like powers, and yet admit that she was a woman and that her power was limited by her subjects, and in particular by Parliament. As Queen she listened to advice, but made her own decisions. As she told Parliament on one occasion, "I will never by violence be constrained to do anything." At another time, when she was referring to the need for Catholics and Protestants to live together, she told members, "I mean to guide them both by God's holy true rule." Her ministers, and indeed her subjects, came to realize that no one could hope to encroach upon the royal prerogative. When she died a popular ballad expressed the general feeling that:

> *She rul'd this Nation by her selfe,*
> > *And was beholden to no man;*
> *O she bore the sway and of all affairs,*
> > *And yet she was but a woman.*

Both as Queen and woman, Elizabeth became a legend in her lifetime. At home, whatever doubts some may have had about the monarchy, she commanded the respect and loyalty of her subjects. Abroad she was regarded as a symbol of feminine magnificence and national greatness. The Frenchman, De Maisse, called her "a great prince, whom nothing escapes." Actress she may have been—the stately ceremonial which surrounded her person far exceeded that of any other court in Europe—but she was a real mistress of statecraft, capable of uniting and harnessing the energy and enterprise of her people who for the first time were realizing a national identity.

Under her Stuart successors the clever personal compromise, which was the secret of Elizabeth's success, gave way to the Divine Right of Kings—a doctrine whereby the monarch existed by the will of God, and not merely by the will of the people or the consent of Parliament. Conflict then became inevitable and civil war eventually ensued.

In Elizabethan England the government of the realm was carried on at the royal court by the Queen (page 44), assisted by the Privy Council. Although Parliament was accepted as "the most high and absolute power of the realm of England" it was only called when necessary (41). Queen Elizabeth exercized almost complete authority in administering its laws and conducting her own foreign policy. She never hesitated to forbid discussion of topics which she regarded as beyond Parliament's province.

The decision to send troops to the Netherlands under the command of the Earl of Leicester, for example, was entirely hers. Similarly she defied Parliament's wishes in the matter of her marriage and succession, though when the need for money arose she quickly had recourse to Parliament. This exercize of personal authority relied in practice on the devoted service of a group of experienced servants of state who, like the Queen, were interested in furthering the country's welfare. Elizabeth

was well served by a number of outstanding ministers, of whom the greatest was William Cecil, later Lord Burghley, who held the offices of Principal Secretary of State and Lord Treasurer (42). Other influential ministers were Sir Francis Walsingham (43), who from 1570 was employed mostly in foreign affairs, and Robert Cecil, Secretary of State from 1596, who followed his father in becoming the most powerful English statesman of his day. The Queen too had her favourites and balanced off one against another. Chief among them were Robert Dudley, Earl of Leicester (44), who after being the chief object of Elizabeth's affections died in disgrace in 1588 after exceeding his authority in the Netherlands. Others were Sir Christopher Hatton, who became Chancellor; the unstable Earl of Essex (45), who went to the scaffold for rebellion in 1601; and Sir Walter Raleigh, whose fortunes collapsed when he married one of the Queen's maids of honour.

26 One of Elizabeth's greatest political virtues was that, despite her independent temperament, she managed the country's affairs in such a way that most of her subjects came to accept her will as theirs. Fully alive to the dangers—political, religious and economic—that might have undermined her position and the safety of her beloved England, she used her consummate tact, skill and equivocation in a manner which not only consolidated her rule but won for her the contentment of her people.

Despite long correspondence about the art of kingship between Elizabeth and James VI of Scotland, as he then was, James's accession (46) to the English throne in 1603 marked a turning point in the relationship of monarchy and Parliament. By the time he became King of England James regarded himself, in his own words, as "an experienced king, needing no lessons." Modesty was certainly not one of this ruler's virtues. Indeed his arrogance and actions—based on a belief in the doctrine of

46

47

ROBERTUS CAR COMES SOMERSET VICE COMES ROFFENSIS AUREÆ PERISCEL EQVES.

Charles Pri

49

R.B. *sculp.*

48

the Divine Right of Kings—were soon to involve him in a series of disputes with Parliament which ultimately would end in the execution of his son, Charles I. Elizabeth had been cautious in the choice of her servants and slow even to the extent of meanness in rewarding service; James made the opposite mistake. After Robert Cecil's death in 1612 James fell under the influence of favourites and showered titles and rewards on courtiers and handsome young men. His first favourite, Robert Carr, Earl of Somerset, was condemned to death for his part in a murder (47). Though reprieved by the King, he was supplanted by George Villiers, who as Duke of Buckingham (48) was to exercize such tragic influence over Prince Charles, who succeeded his father in 1625 (49). It is interesting to speculate whether the course of events might have been different if James's first son, Henry had lived to be King (50).

50

Queen Elizabeth's Court moved about from palace to palace and on "progresses" during the summer, stopping at the homes of courtiers who, though flattered, could be almost bankrupted by the lavish hospitality. The Queen's progresses reminded her subjects of her majestic dignity. She "appeared like a goddess such as painters are wont to depict" (51). Henry Machyn, merchant taylor of the City of London, recorded that: "the 25th day of April was St. Mark's day, the Queen's grace supped at Baynard Castle at my Lord of Pembroke's place, and after supper the Queen's grace rowed up and down the Thames, and a hundred boats about her grace, with trumpets and drums and flutes and guns, and squibs hurling on high to and fro . . . and all the water-side stood with a thousand people looking on her

51

52

53

grace" (52). The Queen's most memorable progress was the Earl of Leicester's entertainment at Kenilworth Castle (53) in 1575. For eighteen days the royal guests enjoyed lavish banquets and spectacular entertainments, ending with a water pageant. The same magnificence characterized Queen Elizabeth's funeral procession (page 45). James I's Court was even more glamorous by reason of the extravagant masques devised by Ben Jonson and Inigo Jones to delight Queen Anne of Denmark. Perhaps the spirit of the age was best exemplified in Inigo Jones' Banqueting House at Whitehall (page 45), his Queen's House at Greenwich (54), the rooms at Wilton House, or the Queen's chapel at St. James's Palace (55).

55

54

The High Court of Parliament played a major part in Tudor government. Sir Thomas Smyth, who had been Secretary of State in 1548 and 1572 and had served as royal ambassador several times, wrote in 1583: "The most high and absolute power of the realm of England consisteth in the Parliament. For every Englishman is intended to be there present, either in person or by procuration and attornies, of what pre-eminence, state, dignity or quality soever he be, from the Prince (be he King or Queen) to the lowest person of England." This was the theory, and in essence the Parliament of Elizabeth and James was what it had been since the Middle Ages—the monarch in council with the peers (56) of the realm, and with Commons in attendance at the bar of the chamber (57). This tradition is still maintained in the state opening of Parliament by the sovereign; but although ceremonial may have changed little over the centuries the authority of the ruler from the

56

throne in the House of Lords has passed to the opposite end of the Palace of Westminster. Perhaps the most outstanding figure associated with Parliament and the law during this period was Sir Edward Coke (58). He was an eminent judge and legal writer, best remembered for his *Reports* and *Institutes* which profoundly influenced English law. Under Elizabeth he held various public offices, including that of Speaker of the House of Commons and Attorney-General. Under James I he championed the cause of common law and Parliament against the Church and the royal prerogative. With great personal courage he threw the weight of his immense legal experience and influence on the side of Parliament against arbitrary personal Government and set an example which influenced John Pym (59) and his colleagues to stand firm against Charles I.

57

58

59

The authority of the Court and Parliament was projected into the country as a whole through the highly efficient local administration which Elizabeth (60) inherited from her predecessors. The Council of the North was responsible for maintaining peace and order beyond the River Trent, while in the border country near Wales there was the Council of the Marches, based on Ludlow and Shrewsbury in Shropshire, with Sir Henry Sidney as its Lord President. The chief administrative unit, however, remained the county. Here the Lord Lieutenant as the monarch's personal representative was at its head. With the help of deputies, Justices of the Peace and other officers he ruled the countryside. With the political dangers of the time and as the activities of central government expanded, these local officers came to play an important role. The Lords Lieutenant were frequently peers and privy counsellors, such as Lord Burghley himself or the Earl of Pembroke (61). Pem-

60

broke was responsible not only for his home counties of Somerset and Wiltshire but for all the Welsh counties and Marches (borderlands) where his family held estates. Generally speaking, the other people involved in local administration—Justices of the Peace, sheriffs, coroners, high constables and overseers—were drawn from the ranks of the local rural gentry. They performed a variety of duties assigned to them to ensure the preservation of order, the execution of justice and the military security of the community. The Lord Lieutenant, with his deputies, was responsible for holding the musters of the shire (i.e. checking the number of armed men available) (62, 63), selecting officers and men for the trained bands, and assembling warlike equipment. The Justices of the Peace exercized judicial functions, fixed wages and prices, supervized the levying of the poor rate, and enforced statutes and proclamations from time to time.

61

62

63

Long before Queen Elizabeth came to the throne the Church in England had experienced a long period of unrest. In the last years of Edward III the reformer John Wycliffe and his followers (the Lollards) had demanded Church services in English instead of Latin, and had translated the Bible into English. During the fifteenth century adherents to Lollardy continued to urge reform in religious observance. Inspired by the Protestant teaching of Martin Luther in Germany, and John Calvin in Switzerland, a number of eminent divines incurred royal displeasure for their persistent advocacy of Protestant ideas. Thomas Bilney (64) was burned to death in 1531 and the bodies of Martin Bucer and Paul Fagius, both Cambridge divines who had advocated reform, were solemnly exhumed under Mary in 1557 and burned on Market Hill (65). In 1534 Henry VIII had severed the English Church from Rome, and dissolved the monasteries in 1536–39. Religious changes

followed and in 1538 the English Bible issued by Archbishop Cranmer (66) was ordered to be read in every parish church. Yet at the same time Henry encouraged Charles V to seek out William Tyndale, who had translated the Bible, and execute him (67). English Protestants were arrested and burned to death. Under Edward VI (1547–53) the Prayer Book was issued in English instead of Latin and in 1552 articles of Protestant belief were made binding on the clergy. There followed the period of stern Catholic reaction under Queen Mary (1553–58). Among the many Protestant martyrs (68) were John Rogers, who had helped to translate the Bible, and Bishops Latimer, Ridley and Cranmer. It is not surprising that at Elizabeth's accession both Catholics and Protestants alike fearfully awaited some sign of her policy.

68

66

At Elizabeth's accession in 1558 the ministers and bishops of Mary were still in power and had support from abroad. The returning Protestant exiles were eager for reforms more far-reaching than under Edward VI (69). Elizabeth disliked them both, for the Catholics regarded her as illegitimate and might be prepared to plot against her, and the Puritans were opposed to bishops, whom Elizabeth regarded as essential for upholding the mon-

archy. Unlike Mary (70), she decided on a policy of compromise. This was expressed in the Acts of Supremacy and Uniformity in 1559 and a statement of doctrine embodied in the Thirty Nine Articles of 1563. In general terms the settlement denied Papal authority in the country and imposed moderate Protestantism, requiring the use of the Second Prayer book of Edward VI with significant changes. Only one of Mary's bishops accepted this, and most went

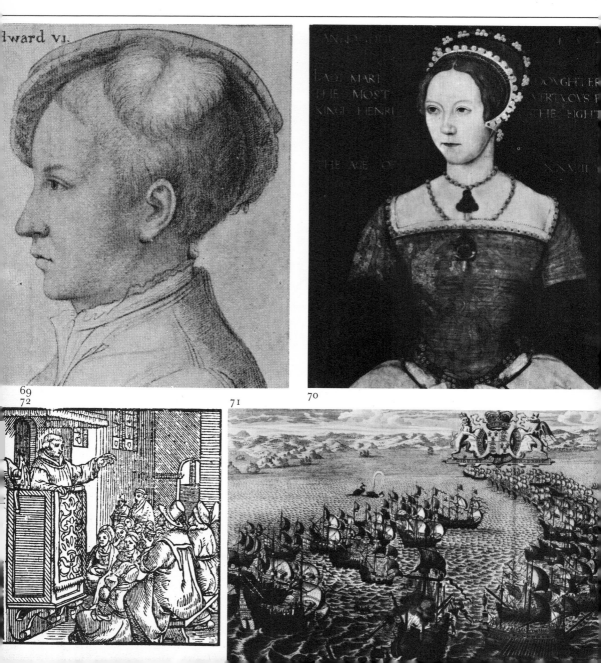

69

70

72

71

to prison. Parish priests refusing to conform were deprived of their livings and Catholics were fined for non-attendance at church. Sterner measures, including execution, were later taken after Elizabeth had been excommunicated by the Pope in 1570, and as the presence of Mary Queen of Scots, Catholic and heir apparent, and the Spanish Armada (71), seemed to endanger the Queen's position. Puritan clergy who refused to wear the Church vestments required by the law were similarly removed. The Queen's dislike of the Puritans showed itself in her displeasure against preachers (72). The ability to preach was no recommendation for royal favour, though preaching—St. Paul's Cross was a favourite place for open air sermons—was coming to be seen as essential to the reformed faith (73).

In spite of plots against her life, and the threat of the Spanish Armada in 1588, Queen Elizabeth's reign proved to be a time during which the position of the monarchy was considerably strengthened. Following the accession of James I in 1603 the Catholics looked forward to changes in their favour, especially to some relaxation in the penalties levied against them. It was known that James was more tolerant than most rulers of his day; he had made himself unpopular with extreme Protestants by refusing to send recusants to the scaffold. Nevertheless he made no attempt to alter the severe laws against the Catholics, and many still suffered for their faith. It was because of this and in despair of securing concessions by peaceful means that a group of recusant Catholics (74) turned to treason. Led by Robert Catesby, a Warwickshire gentleman, they devised a plot to blow up the King, Lords and Commons when Parliament met on 5th November, 1605. Guy Fawkes, an old

74

77

soldier in the Spanish service, was hired to detonate the gunpowder hidden in the cellars under the House of Lords at the appointed time (75). The Catholic gentry of the Midlands were to rise in support of a plan to seize the King's daughter, Elizabeth, who would then become a Catholic Queen. Robert Cecil's spies unearthed the plot the day before. Fawkes was arrested and tortured (76). Catesby was killed while attempting to resist arrest, and the other conspirators were executed (77). The immediate result of the Gunpowder Plot was to produce even harsher measures against the recusants. The years that followed were marked by religious unrest and intrigue and growing constitutional difficulties as the relations between King and Parliament deteriorated. Nor did the marriage of the Prince of Wales (the future Charles I) to Catholic princess Henrietta Maria, sister of King Louis XIII of France, bring any hope of unity.

75

76

Calais, England's last European possession, had been lost to the French under Queen Mary (1553–59). Elizabeth's shrewd policy during her early years was to hold the balance between France, and the Spain of Philip II (78), playing off Protestant against Catholic. Philip's attempt to crush Protestantism in the Netherlands, which inspired Bruegel's painting, *The Massacre of the Innocents,* only served to evoke English sympathy for the rebels (page 46). When England allied herself to France, the struggle entered a more bitter phase. Sir Martin Frobisher (page 47) was ordered by the Queen to make reprisals on Spanish ports. In 1588, Spain's great Armada entered the English Channel (79). After a running fight lasting nearly a week, the English ships (80) bore down on the Spanish fleet off Gravelines, where a decisive battle was fought. Few Spanish galleons managed to escape. This victory medal was struck the following year (81).

78

79

80

81

Shakespeare's monument in Holy Trinity Church, Stratford, was erected by the time the First Folio was published in 1623 (page 10)

Above An open-air performance in a Flemish village, painted
by Jan Bruegel (page 14)

Right Guests at Sir Henry Unton's wedding feast being
entertained by masquers and musicians playing the flute and
viols (page 16)

FRANCE

whicwon

43

44

Left Queen Elizabeth I in ceremonial dress. She governed the realm from her royal court and exercized almost complete authority in administering laws and conducting foreign policy (page 24)

Right The Banqueting House, designed by Inigo Jones. Charles I commissioned the splendid ceiling by Rubens in memory of his father (page 29)

Below Queen Elizabeth's funeral procession (1603) characterized the same magnificence as the lavish banquets and spectacular entertainments held during her reign (page 29)

45

Left Bruegel's famous painting, *The Massacre of the Innocents*, shows the Duke of Alva's men mercilessly crushing the Dutch Protestant rebellion (page 40)

Right Sir Martin Frobisher, a famed navigator in his day, played a leading role in the defeat of the Spanish Armada (page 40)

Sir Christopher Hatton, Queen Elizabeth's Lord Chancellor,
dressed in a fashionable doublet and accessories (page 71)

London Bridge in Shakespeare's day—with wooden buildings
used as shops and the splendid houses of wealthy merchants
perched on top (page 64)

Above The Lord Mayor of London with his attendants (page 66)

Below An Elizabethan water carrier with his dog (page 73)

Left Compton Wynyates, a great house in Warwickshire, which shows a combination of medieval and Tudor architecture (page 85)

Above Hall's Croft, Stratford. The home of Dr. John Hall and his wife Susanna, Shakespeare's elder daughter (page 89)

Hunters and hounds outside Nonsuch Palace, Surrey (page 96)

The departure of an English East Indiamen on a trading
voyage. Ships like these established the East India Company as
"the pioneer of imperial England in the East" (page 105)

longtain voyage: quil souffra de porter seulemet ung
las de soye a ung ymage de sainct george pendat a icelluy.
Aussi se ledit colier dor auoit besoing de reparacion il pora
estre mise en la main de louurier iusques a ce quil soit
repare. Lequel colier aussi ne pourra estre enrichy de
pierres ou daultres choses reserue les ymage qui pourra
estre garny au plaisir du cheualier. Et taussi ne pourra
estre ledit colier vendu engaige donne ne aliene pour
necessite ou cause quelconque que ce soit

Alexander Rex Scoto𝔯𝔦

Lewellin princeps Wallie

Left The Lord Chancellor and the principal officers of the crown seated on a woolsack in the House of Lords. They are flanked by the clergy and nobility (page 108)

Above Sir Francis Drake and Sir John Hawkins sailed on their daring expeditions in ships very similar to these (page 117)

ALTISSIMVS
CREAVIT DE TERRA MEDECYNAMET VIR
PRVDENS NON ABHOREBIT ILLAM
ANNO DOMMINI 1623

Surgical operations were still a hazard in Shakespeare's time.
This medical practitioner's signboard shows the many
operations which the surgeon was prepared to carry out (page
122)

Following the example of Elizabeth, James I believed that English foreign policy should be conducted by the Crown. As a lover of peace, James made terms with Spain in 1604. He later began negotiations for the marriage of his son, Prince Charles, to the Infanta Maria, the daughter of Philip III of Spain. Lured on by the prospect of the discovery of treasure, James was persuaded to sponsor Sir Walter Raleigh's (82) expedition to South America. James was reluctant to involve himself in Europe's Thirty Years' War (1618–48), but eventually he agreed that Prince Charles and Buckingham should go to Madrid (83) to woo the Infanta and win Spanish support for the Elector Palatine's cause. The mission failed, and James was delighted to welcome the return of his son (84) without the Infanta. The final rebuff to Spain was England's alliance with France, brought about by Charles's marriage in 1625 to Maria, sister of King Louis XIII (85).

83

85

During Shakespeare's lifetime people of all degrees, from the sovereign downwards, firmly believed in witchcraft. According to Sir Edward Coke, the lawyer, a witch was "a person who hath conference with the Devil, to consult with him or to do some act," usually, it may be added, of an evil kind (86). Even the enlightened Bishop Jewel, preaching before Queen Elizabeth in 1572 claimed to have seen "most evident and manifest marks of their wickedness" and urged that the laws touching such evil-doers should be put into execution. Alongside the fairies, their friendlier counterparts, witches were to be found throughout the countryside. Frederick, Duke of Württemberg, who visited England in 1592, observed that "many witches are found there, who frequently do much mischief by means of hail and tempests." Enlightened writers like Reginald Scot in his *The Discoverie of Witchcraft* (1584) tried to expose the fallacy of belief in witchcraft and sorcery. But equally reputable theo-

87

91

86

90

Anne Baker   Ioane Willmott   Ellen Greene

logians like George Gifford, though adopting a commonsense attitude towards witches, did not deny their existence. James I himself, who was fascinated by psychic phenomena, certainly feared witches and expressed his views in his *Daemonologie*. Although Shakespeare probably believed little in witchcraft he makes Joan of Arc a witch and opens *Macbeth* with the three witches (inspired by Holinshed's "three women in strange and wild apparell, resembling creatures of elder world"). Many

Jacobean writers refer to the black art in their plays and poems. The most famous witch case of the period concerned the four women of North Berwick in Scotland, who were accused, sentenced and burned to death for conspiring to destroy James VI (then King of Scotland) and his Queen, in 1591 (87). The more fortunate of suspected witches escaped with punishment of the ducking stool (88, 89), but many, like the three witches of Belvoir in 1619 (90), were burned in public (91).

CHAPTER THREE

A CHANGING REALM

SHAKESPEARE'S ENGLAND had two sovereigns—Elizabeth I and James I—but only one sovereign city, as William Dunbar, the Scottish poet, had written much earlier in the sixteenth century in his poem *In Honour of the City of London*:

London, thou art of townes A per se.
Sovereign of cities, seemliest in sight,
Of high renown, riches and royalty;
Of lords, barons and many a goodly knight;
Of most delectable lusty ladies bright;
Of famous prelates, in habits clerical;
Of merchants full of substance and of might:
London, thou art the flower of cities all.

Dunbar had accompanied the Scottish ambassadors to the Court of Henry VII (1485–1509) during the negotiations for the marriage of the King's daughter, Margaret Tudor, to the future James IV of Scotland—a union which eventually resulted in the accession of James VI of Scotland as King James I of England in 1603. The Scottish Court at that time was by no means uncultured, but Dunbar was obviously impressed with what he saw in London.

Most foreign visitors to England's capital during Elizabeth's reign were similarly struck, as evidenced by the descriptions of several of them that have survived. If Whitehall and Westminster were added to the City, then London was by far the biggest city of England and the largest capital in Europe. Though it had squalor as well as splendour Shakespeare's London was generally considered "an ornament to the realm by the beauty

thereof," while the Thames with its one bridge gave it a unique character and appeal. Englishmen regarded their capital as a proud city, providing a focal point of national life centred upon the splendour of the Court, the wealth and commercial activities of the merchants, the law and Parliament, literature and the arts, the theatre and popular entertainment, not to mention the latest trends in fashion and manners. One contemporary writer regarded London as "that adamant which draweth unto it all the other parts of the land"; but there was the opposite view that the real life of England centred upon its country towns and villages, fields and mansions. The poet and essayist, Sir Thomas Overbury (1581–1613) wrote of the country gentleman whom it was almost impossible to attract to London: "And when he is there, he sticks fast upon every object, casts his eyes away upon gazing, and becomes the prey of every cutpurse. When he comes home, those wonders serve him for his holiday talk."

The countryman clearly could learn much from what he found in the busy capital. Here was a mixed society depending for its security and prosperity upon observance of "degree," as often expressed by Shakespeare. There was no idea of democracy as now known. The social system was based upon an acceptance of rank, this being the guarantee of the stability which allowed the commercial enterprise of the merchant class. Men and women at all levels of society had their virtues and failings, then as now; and it is not surprising that in an age of keen competition and change there were aspects of life which drew critics. Thomas Nash, the satirist, wrote in 1593: "In London, the rich disdain the poor. The courtier the citizen. The citizen the countryman. One occupation disdaineth another. The merchant the retailer. The retailer the craftsman. The better sort of craftsman the baser. The shoemaker the cobbler. The cobbler the carman. One nice dame disdains her next door neighbour should have that furniture to her house, or dainty duck or device, which she wants. She will not go to church, because she disdains to mix herself with base company, and cannot have her close pew by herself."

Nevertheless, to the foreigner, the capital stood as the symbol of England's greatness. Visiting it in 1592, Frederick Duke of Wurtëmberg described it as "a large, excellent and mighty city of business, and the most important in the whole kingdom." He was immensely impressed by the commercial activities of its inhabitants and the shipping in the Thames. It was "a very prosperous city," he observed, "so that one can scarcely pass along the streets, on account of the throng." His impression was that the inhabitants were "magnificently apparel-led, and are extremely proud and overbearing; and because the greater part, especially the tradespeople, seldom go into other countries, but always remain in their houses in the city attending to their business, they care little for foreigners, but scoff and laugh at them." Street boys and apprentices were frequently encountered in groups and often showed little respect to other pedestrians. Women, however, so this foreigner observed, "had much more liberty than perhaps in any other place; they also know how to make use of it, for they go out in exceedingly fine clothes, and give all their attention to their ruffs and stuffs, to such a degree indeed, that, as I am informed, many a one does not hesitate to wear velvet in the streets, which is common with them, whilst at home perhaps they have not a piece of dry bread."

This picture of London reflected, though on an exaggerated scale, what was happening in the country as a whole. The unsettled years of the Wars of the Roses had passed and Elizabeth's Church settlement had brought compromise to conflicting religious views. With the removal of the fear of foreign invasion following the defeat of the Armada in 1588 a new spirit of self confidence and adventure had begun to permeate national life.

Elizabethan London was described by Thomas Dekker as the "noblest city of the now noblest nation." London was the political and commercial hub of England, a city beloved by its inhabitants and admired by foreign visitors. Its population, estimated to have increased to some 200,000 by the end of Elizabeth's reign, made it possibly the biggest city in Europe. It was at least ten times the size of any other English city. Two contemporary sources enable a detailed and accurate picture of London in the time of Shakespeare to be reconstructed. The first is a picture-map (92)—drawn about 1560, which appeared in the famous continental atlas, *Civitates Orbis Terrarum*, of Braun and Hogenburg, first published at Cologne in 1572. The second is the *Survey of London* (1598, 1603), written by John Stow, a leading antiquary and historian of his time who also compiled the *Annals of England* (1592). The city itself, occupying the area still known as the "City," covered about a square mile in

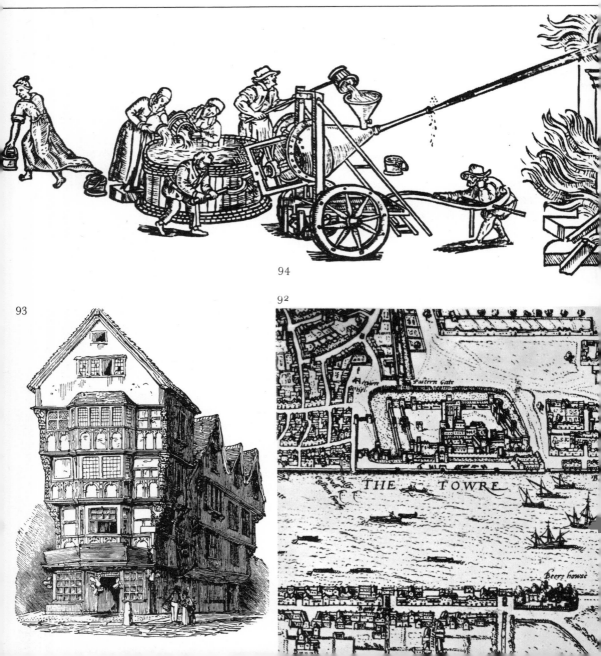

94

93

92

THE TOWRE

extent and lay inside the old Roman and medieval walls. The River Thames formed its southern boundary. Its boundaries and gates can still be traced today in Aldersgate, Cripplegate, Moorgate, Bishopsgate, and Aldgate. Within the city a network of narrow streets, congested with the busy commercial life of the capital, were dominated by tall, timber-framed buildings (93), which constituted a great fire risk (94). These buildings served as shops, warehouses, counting-houses and residences. Outside the walls lay the open countryside, though the built-up area was overflowing on all sides: along the waterfront east of the Tower (95) (the East End); beyond the northern gates, as shown on Norden's map of 1593 (96); westward along the highway of the Strand, to the separate City of Westminster; and across the River to the south, the Borough of Southwark where playhouses and entertainments flourished outside the control of the Puritan City authorities.

"Both for the beauty of building, infinite riches [and] variety of all things" London excelled all the cities in the world. London Bridge, the only bridge across the River Thames, was said by the writer Fynes Moryson, "worthily to be numbered among the miracles of the world." A contemporary painting gives a good impression of the wooden buildings used as shops and "quite splendid, handsome and well-built houses," inhabited by wealthy merchants and haberdashers, perched on the bridge (page 48). Cornelius Visscher's famous map, drawn soon after Elizabeth's death, shows in the foreground St. Mary Overy (Southwark Cathedral) and the Southwark Gate of the bridge, complete with the traitors' heads, put on this gate after 1577 (97). The beautiful medieval cathedral church of St. Paul's, whose graceful spire had fallen a victim to lightning in 1561, dominated the City, and the central aisle of its nave, known as "Paul's Walk," provided a fashionable

97
99

98
100

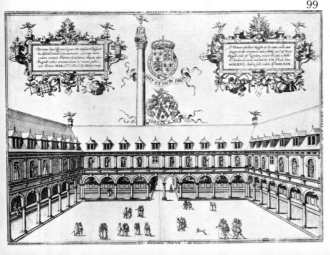

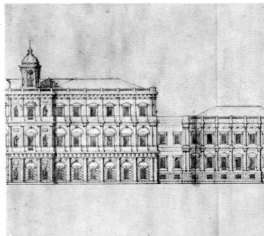

meeting place. Over a hundred lesser church spires rose in every part of the City. The Poultry, formerly the quarter occupied by the poulterers, had by this time given way to grocers, haberdashers and upholsterers. Cheapside, with its Cross (98), had become the City's leading market place where goods of all kinds were displayed and sold. Symbolizing the wider influence of commerce at this period was the Royal Exchange, built in 1571 (99) by Sir Thomas Gresham, merchant and financial adviser to the Queen. Then as now, the houses of the great and the royal palaces similarly attracted attention: the Queen's beloved Whitehall, with its banqueting house built in 1572, later replaced by Inigo Jones in 1619 (100); the riverside mansions of the nobles with their fine gardens near to John of Gaunt's Savoy (101) to the west of the City, and the nucleus of buildings around the Abbey of Westminster and the Parliament House (102, 103).

101   102
103

Sala Regalis cum Curia Westmonastery, vulgo Westminster haall.

66   Long before Shakespeare, London had been self-governing. Its rulers were the Lord Mayor (page 49)—accompanied on ceremonial occasions by the Lady Mayoress (104)—and the Court of Aldermen, wealthy men connected with City commerce and elected by the twenty-six wards or districts into which the City was divided. The Aldermen (105) chose the Lord Mayor each year from their members. The headquarters of government was the Guildhall (106), where procedures, ceremonies and traditions were firmly established. The ward system had been designed to link local responsibilities with those who lived locally. The ward, for instance, was responsible for keeping peace and order, and the citizens themselves were expected to serve in rotation as members of the watch. The picture of Dogberry and his amateur watchmen drawn by Shakespeare in *Much Ado About Nothing* was

104

105   107

inspired by this. There was also the Court of Common Council, which was concerned mostly with by-laws and street regulations. For example, in 1599 it ordered householders to hang lanterns in front of their houses at specified times as a form of street lighting, and organized bellmen or night watchmen to call the hours (107) and cresset-bearers to light the way (108). The real power, however, lay with the Court of Aldermen, responsible for the many prisons, finance, elections, and legal work. Then, as now, the Lord Mayor took precedence over all save the sovereign and to assist him in the discharge of his duties he had the help of an executive officer, the Sheriff, with his Under-sheriff and bailiff or catch-pole (109).

106

108

109

68

The Elizabethan period saw a "general amendment of lodging" among nobility, gentry, and the lowest classes too. The great hall of medieval times gave way to smaller chambers (110) and panelled rooms (111). Fireplaces and glazed windows became more common and the use of wall and ceiling decoration, wainscotting and carved features introduced colour and variety, as did tapes-tries, carpets and painted cloths. Basic furniture was still scanty—tables, settles, coffers, cupboards, joint stools and a few chairs, some with embroidered covers. As to sleeping arrangements, the luxury of the time was the great curtained four-poster bed with its warming pan (112, 113). The servants and lowest classes had simple truckle beds or straw pallets. Each house had its kitchen equipment

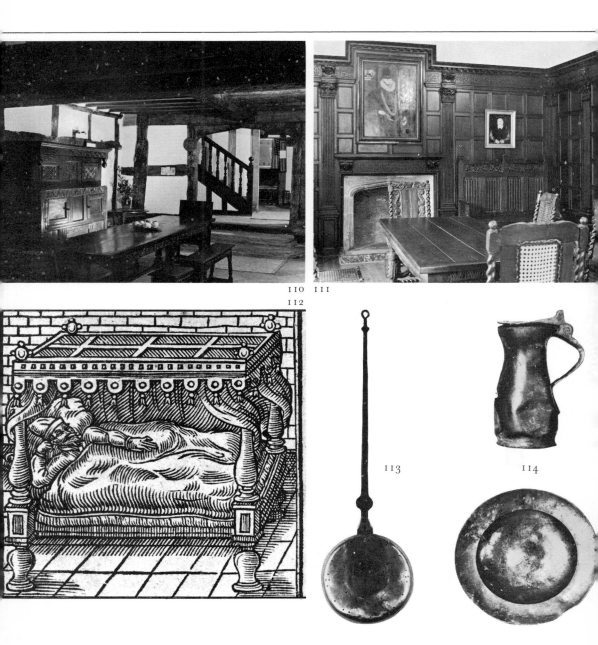

110 111
112

113   114

and plate (114). Although sanitation was primitive, the upper classes washed and bathed—possibly not often—using soap and perfume. Habits of eating and drinking followed a common pattern. Breakfast, often taken privately by the great, could be quite substantial, but the main meal was dinner, generally taken towards the end of the morning. Supper came in the early evening (115). Poor folk ate from bare tables using wooden or pewter dishes, though earthenware dishes and tankards were common (116). A rich table was covered with a cloth, and a trencher, knife and spoon provided for each place, together with glass bowls (117), goblets, ivory knife holders (118), linen napery and salts (119).

116   117   118   119

Few periods in English history have seen greater extravagance of dress than the Elizabethan age. Queen Elizabeth herself gave a lead to her ladies in embroidered brocade farthingale dresses, as in the Ditchley portrait of Elizabeth (120), while the gentlemen vied with them with their colourful, finely decorated doublets, breeches and accessories. The picture depicting the *Procession of Queen Elizabeth to Blackfriars* in the City gives a vivid impression of the colourful elegance of courtiers' dress. Even "the Ploughman, that in times past was contented in russet, must nowadays have his doublet of the fashion with wide cuts, his garters of fine silk of Granado to meet his Sis on Sunday." Splendid examples of

120

Elizabethan garments may be seen at the Victoria and Albert Museum and at the London Museum (121). Portraits of the period also provide excellent illustrations, for example that of Sir Christopher Hatton, who became Elizabeth's Lord Chancellor (page 48). The sketches by Hoefnagel illustrate the distinction between a rich London merchant's clothes and those of a young man, a young noblewoman and a commoner (122). Footwear, gloves (123), and jewellery were fashionable accessories. Even gentlemen wore jewels (124): Raleigh, for instance, wore pearl earrings and a row of pearls on his fur-lined coat.

121

122

124

123

72 Englishmen knew how to enjoy their leisure. Many sports, such as hunting the deer and hare, falconry, fowling and angling had a distinctly country flavour. Other sports included bull and bear baiting, and cockfighting. Organized sport played before large crowds in the modern sense did not exist, but the streets, open fields and inns were often the scene of popular entertainment and games. Football was associated with "people of meaner sort." Dancing and music-making were popular, as were itinerant tumblers, ballad-sellers, and performing animals like Marocco the horse (125). Archery, still officially encouraged for national defence, continued to be fashionable (126). Indeed, a public archery range was provided outside the City walls. The English also enjoyed playing chess (127) and draughts, merels and shovel board, bowls and skittles, dicing and cards. Tennis was played by the courtiers, including the Queen's favourite, Leicester (128).

125   128

126   127

If on your man you light
The first draught shall you play,
If not tis mine by right
At first to lead the way

The Queen herself profited from Drake's attacks on Spain. Landowners came to regard their estates as commercial investments, importing hops, potatoes, and other new fruits and vegetables. Tradesmen and craftsmen flourished and the Statute of Apprentices ensured a supply of skilled labour. In the cities trading companies, and in London the livery companies, controlled manufacture, apprenticeship and selling. London was the centre of England's commercial life, and its international status grew apace. There was a brisk demand for cloth and clothing (129), footwear (130), jewellery and similar products. The City too had to be fed, and had special markets in Billingsgate, Smithfield (131), and Cheapside. Hogenberg's map gives an idea of the shops in Cheapside with the stalls and water vessels which were used by professional water-carriers (page 49).

131

Sanitary conditions in Elizabethan England, especially in the cities and towns, were really primitive. Even in London, few rich men had a piped water supply in their homes. Most people relied on wells, cisterns, and water-sellers. Thames water was still drunk, though the risk of pollution must have been great. Only in times of plague was any real attempt made to remove garbage which filled the narrow streets. In Stratford-upon-Avon, Shakespeare's father was fined for leaving a "muckhill" near his house in Henley Street. Summer epidemics were common. Garbage bred flies and, without insecticides, attempts to deal with them were rarely successful (132). Vermin spread the infection, despite the

132 133

134

efforts of rat-catchers (133). In time of plague, theatres and other public places were closed and the rich fled to the country (134). Rules to be followed in "time of pestilence" were circulated among the poor, but did little good (135). For ordinary folk, the funeral procession with the advance warning of its bell, and the sight of search parties looking for corpses in the street, was a common sight (136). Whole households were decimated. In 1563, some 20,000 people died in London, and in 1564, the year of Shakespeare's birth, nearly one-sixth of the people of Stratford perished. Increasing urban prosperity and a growing population brought problems of development which were hard to control.

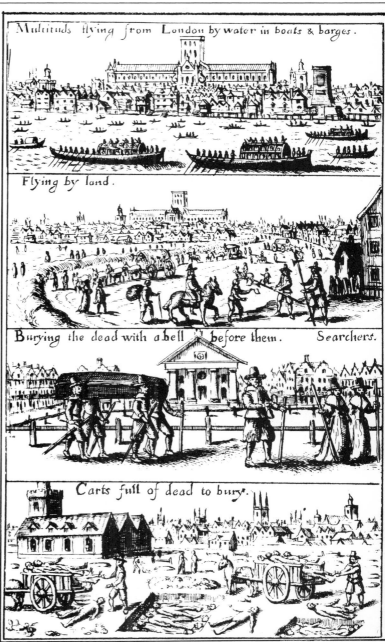

CERTAINE
RVLES,
DIRECTIONS,
OR ADVERTIS-
MENTS FOR THIS
TIME OF PESTILENTI-
ALL CONTAGION:

WITH

A caueat to those that weare about their neckes impoisoned Amulets as a Preseruatiue from the Plague:

First published for the behoofe of the City of London in the last visitation, 1603. And now reprinted for the said Citie, and all other parts of the Land at this time visited; by FRANCIS HERING, D. in Physicke, and Fellow of the Colledge of Physitians in LONDON.

Whereunto is added certaine Directions, for the poorer sort of people when they shall be visited.

16. Num. 47.

And Aaron *tooke as Moyses commanded, and ranne into the midst of the congregation: and behold the plague was begun among the people, and he put on incense, and made an atonement for the people.*

LONDON,
Printed by WILLIAM IONES.
1625.

136

In Shakespeare's day the "broad River of Thames," as an Italian visitor called it, served as a highway for the City, the country and the world at large. In 1592 Duke Frederick of Würtemberg was impressed by the commercial activity of London. The River was "most useful and convenient for this purpose, considering that ships from France, the Netherlands, Sweden, Denmark, Hamburg and other kingdoms, come almost up to the city, to which they convey goods and receive and take away others in exchange." Sailing up river from Greenwich, the French Ambassador wrote, "from thence to London it is a magnificent sight to see the number of ships and boats which lie at anchor, insomuch that for two leagues you see nothing but ships that serve as well as for war as for traffic" (137). In the days before taxicabs plied London streets businessmen and visitors often travelled by water on

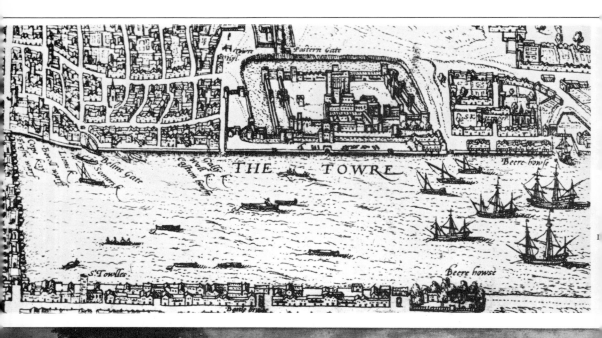

their local journeys. Then as now, London Bridge, a magnificent structure, marked a division in the accessibility of the River. There was a drawbridge in the centre to let ships through, but the narrowness of the space between the piers created a fast current which was a serious navigational hazard. The main shipping basin therefore was the stretch of water immediately below the bridge. Upstream the traffic was less commercial, comprising boats conveying local produce, citizens with their goods, officials on state business, or the rich paying visits. Every great house had its own watergate, and Inigo Jones designed one for the Duke of Buckingham which is all that survives of his house (138). Westward the Thames led on to Richmond (139), and eventually to Windsor (140).

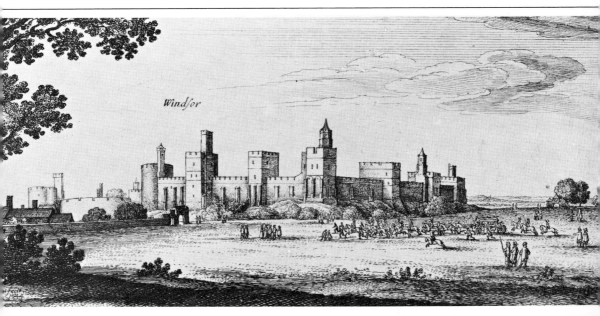

Windsor

139

138

78 All available evidence suggests that travelling by road in Shakespeare's England was an uncomfortable and hazardous business. For most people there was little need to journey from one place to another; many spent their lives without ever moving more than a few miles from their homes. No one travelled for holidays or recreation in the modern sense. On the other hand, business and professional needs involved a good deal of movement to and from the capital, whilst the Queen and her Court, as indeed some noble families, often moved away from the capital making progresses into the country. The great problem was the condition of the roads. Outside the capital and the towns and cities, with the exception of the old Roman roads linking London with Dover, Plymouth, Bristol, Chester and Berwick, the highways were exceedingly bad. Though the poorer folk went on foot, riding on horseback provided the best means of travel (141). As a protection against

141 142

143 144

cold and mud ladies usually wore a cloak and a skirt called a safeguard (143). Along the main roads the provision of post-horses, relays of which stood ready for service at fixed stops, linked with wayside inns which enjoyed a good reputation for food and lodging, made the traveller's task easier. Wheeled carts and packhorses also transported goods to and from London from country places. Farming folk often carried their own produce to and from market in panniers on horseback (142).

Coaches were in little use, except around the capital or as part of the royal trains used by the Queen when she journeyed into the country. The well known picture of Elizabeth arriving at Nonesuch, the great palace that has since entirely disappeared, illustrates transportation at its highest level (145). For the Queen's humbler subjects travel was less comfortable and less safe. Highway robbers and vagabonds took every opportunity to pilfer the ill-prepared traveller (144).

CHAPTER FOUR
SOCIAL LIFE

ELIZABETHAN LONDON, like the age it mirrored, was full of contradictions. Magnificent palaces, stately homes of noblemen, spacious gardens and pleasure grounds; narrow dirty streets with closely-built slum houses lacking privacy and light; the noise of trade and traffic, the cries of street vendors and the sound of sheep and cattle being driven to market; the chiming of bells from City churches; the sweet strains of the flute and notes of the harpsichord within; bare-footed beggars and gay young gallants in their latest colourful attire; vagabonds in rags and ladies in their finery and perfumed wigs; bull and bear-baiting, the theatre and spectacular Court masques; rustics from the country and foreign visitors of State. Everywhere rich splendour in many directions matched by miserable degradation, smells and dirt; yet a peculiar sense of unity and acceptance of class distinction.

London had its disadvantages as well as its delights. During Shakespeare's lifetime, for example, as the City's population grew so did the threat from plague and fire. Many Stratford families were decimated by plague in 1564, and violent epidemics broke out in London in 1593 and 1603. The theatres closed down, and the players escaped to earn a scanty living on tour. Noble families and rich merchants evacuated, as they always did, to their country estates. Indeed, even under normal conditions, there was constant coming and going between the City and the country. England was still predominantly a rural nation; every town had its fields and open spaces and most townsmen felt a natural affinity toward the open countryside.

Queen Elizabeth herself frequently left London on "progresses", transferring her Court with its retinue of courtiers and servants and baggage train of laden carts to chosen country houses and towns, there to enjoy lodging and hospitality for a night or a few days as the case might be. Houses on the grand scale were needed to provide accommodation for the Court. Elizabeth's ministers and nobles built them in rivalry with each other, thereby hoping to achieve fame and advancement in the Queen's service. It was an age of palatial houses embodying new ideas of privacy and comfort and with lavish furnishings far removed from the draughty castle homes of the medieval barons.

The ideas of the planners and architects of these country mansions were clearly influenced by the nature and function of the royal palaces, of which the Queen had a goodly number—Greenwich, Hampton Court, Windsor, Richmond, Nonsuch and the rambling Palace of Whitehall. In addition to these James I showed a great deal of interest in Oatlands in Surrey, which Henry VIII had acquired and rebuilt; it was later renovated by Inigo Jones and became a favourite residence of both Anne of Denmark, consort of James I, and Henrietta Maria, consort of Charles I. Theobalds in Essex, and Newmarket, were also entrusted to Inigo Jones, the latter often being visited by James in company with his favourite George Villiers whom he had made Duke of Buckingham.

In contrast to the splendour of the palaces and the country houses of the men, craftsmen and farming people were simple and scantily furnished. Judged by our standards living conditions were uncomfortable and sanitation in the modern sense did not exist. Food was basic and for the poorer classes represented little more than a subsistence diet. Health was precarious, childbirth and childhood involving serious risks. The family unit was all important and the authority of its head was recognized by custom, law and religion. Discipline was strict and children and servants were liable to be punished at pleasure. The writer John Aubrey (1626–97), looking back to this time, recalled the harshness that was displayed in the home: "The gentry and citizens had little learning of any kind and their way of breeding up their children was suitable to the rest. They were as severe to their children as their schoolmasters, and their schoolmasters were as severe as masters of the house of correction. The child perfectly loathed the sight of his parents as the slave to his torture. Gentlemen of thirty or forty years old were to stand like mutes and fools bareheaded before their parents, and their daughters (well grown women) were to stand at the cupboard-side during the whole time of the proud mother's visits unless (as the fashion was) leave was forsooth desired that a cushion should be given them to kneel upon, brought them by a serving man, after that they had done sufficient penance in standing."

And yet this same age produced some of the most beautiful love poetry in the English language. Shakespeare's sonnets and Donne's compositions cover the whole spectrum of human emotions, from the sheer exhilaration of love in Donne's *Good-Morrow*:

I wonder by my troth, what thou and I
Did, till we lov'd? were we not wean'd till then?

to the cynical despair of Shakespeare's

My love is as a fever, longing still
For that which longer nurseth the disease . . .

The Elizabethans and Jacobeans knew the force of emotions well. Although the stiff and studied portraits of the time may not have suggested this, people cherished deep personal feelings about each other as well as about their religion, country and sovereign.

Everyone was impressed by the magnificence and beauty of the royal palaces, referring to the rich furnishings, pictures, tapestries, embroidery, musical instruments and interior decorative features of gold and silver. Unlike some of her ministers Elizabeth herself built no palaces, but like her father Henry VIII she spent a small fortune modernizing Windsor Castle (146). The chief place of royal residence was Whitehall Palace which had been reconstructed by Henry VIII. The main buildings and garden, including the great hall where plays were performed, lay alongside the River, and the road from Westminster to the City passed between two gatehouses, the northern one by Holbein (147), over which galleries led to various lodgings, the cockpit, tennis court and tilt yard. Whitehall was usually Elizabeth's winter residence, but in summer she installed her Court down the

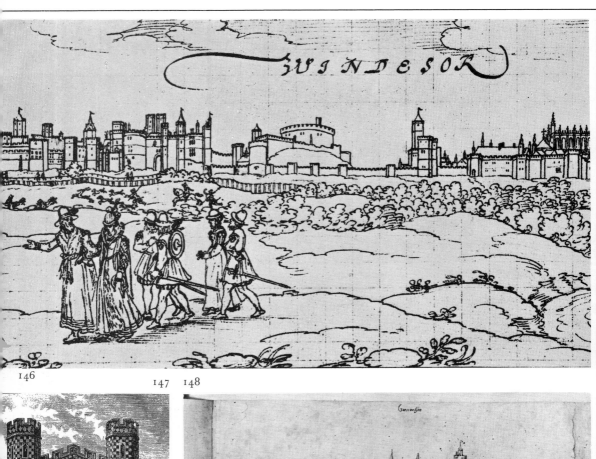

146

147   148

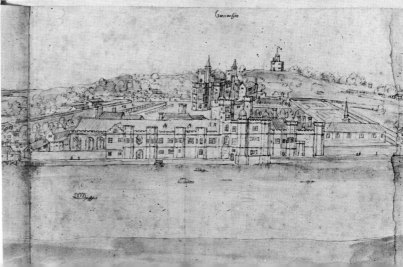

River at Greenwich where at the Palace of Placentia, the site now covered over by the Naval College, she was born (148). Up the River were more palaces: Richmond where Elizabeth died in 1603 and which James I gave to Henry, Prince of Wales (149); and Hampton Court originally built by Cardinal Wolsey who gave it to Henry VIII (150). Elizabeth apparently took a dislike to Hampton after she had an attack of smallpox there in 1562, but it was convenient in times of plague. James I went there during the plague of 1603–4, and the King's Men staged seven performances there. The other palace which the Queen favoured was Nonsuch, though it was too small to house her retinue, some of whom had to occupy tents on the lawn. A creation of exquisite beauty and luxury, Nonsuch has completely disappeared (151).

149

150 151

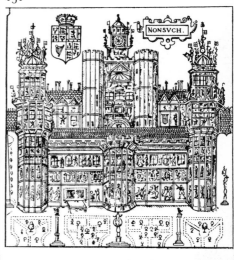

84 Some of England's finest country mansions date back to Elizabeth's reign, inspired by the royal palaces, and the hope that the Queen herself might honour the owners with a royal visit. Men like Lord Burghley and Lord Chancellor Hatton vied with each other, "building for the Queen, building in rivalry with others, building to the limit of their resources and beyond." The great new houses, such as Hatfield House, or Hardwick Hall built by Elizabeth Countess of Shrewsbury in 1590–97, incorporated features such as the tapestried long gallery and great chamber which were ideal for entertaining royal guests, as well as suites of lodgings, parlours and chambers embellished with panelling, decorative pilasters and carving (154). Even the manor houses like the timbered Moreton Old Hall were so provided (152). Considerations of comfort and privacy, rather than those

152
153

of defence and protection, influenced house design. Medieval buildings were adapted, and houses such as Compton Wynyates (page 50) (built 1480 to 1520), show the evolution in progress. The rather solid tower block and the battlements suggest a defensive role, in contrast to the many mullioned windows and elaborate brick chimneys. In Lancashire and Cheshire, elaborate timber-framed houses such as Adlington were built (153). Elsewhere the trend was toward brick and stone, often in Italianate style. Interiors varied in splendour —Buckland Abbey was only average, with its classical pilasters and Renaissance *motif* on the frieze (155). The bedroom from Sizergh Castle in Westmoreland, in the Victoria and Albert Museum, typifies a bedchamber of the period (156).

155

86   Even busy London had close daily ties with the countryside. Sheep were regularly herded through the crowded streets to market (157). Elsewhere the cities and towns were small, and the island as a whole was underpopulated and underdeveloped. Towns like Shakespeare's Stratford-upon-Avon were important for their markets and fairs, serving farmers and country-folk over a wide area. The farmer who came to buy a horse or sell his corn was a familiar figure, as was the visiting country woman with muffler around her mouth (159). Most farm-workers and serving maids rarely left their villages, except once a year to attend a great fair. Farmworkers and maids were customarily hired at one of the hiring fairs, sometimes

57

58

known as "statute fairs" or "mop fairs." Women were expected to stay at home to raise a family, and help with making bread and dairy products, spinning and other practical work (158). Apart from his work in tilling the land to provide subsistence for his family the countryman might sell surplus game (161). In the sixteenth century, age-old rural society began to change. After the dissolution of the monasteries, the conversion of arable into grass land, and the rise of sheep farming, brought wealth to the merchants and landlords but unemployment for thousands of the poorer people, at least until late in Elizabeth's reign (160).

A Countryman

161

159

160

Stratford-upon-Avon typified much of Elizabethan England. Originating as a Roman ford settlement by the River Avon, it became an important crossroads, and centre for markets and fairs. When Shakespeare was born in 1564, Stratford already had centuries of history behind it and, through its trading activities, had wide contacts with the outside world. William Camden called it "a proper little market town." It was a homely town, with a simple layout of streets, houses and shops built mostly of timber from the nearby Forest of Arden. It had "very large streets . . . reasonably well builded of timber." Shakespeare was baptized and also buried in its parish church (162). During the Middle Ages, local affairs had been managed by a powerful guild. After it became a borough in 1553, the town had its own local government. It also had a fine grammar school. Shakespeare's parents both came of farming stock. His father, John, was a glover and wool-dealer by trade,

162

16

16

whose house and shop in Henley Street is now preserved as the Birthplace. John Shakespeare was active in town affairs and was Bailiff of Stratford in 1568. Later he secured a grant of arms (163). Mary Arden, the poet's mother, came of an old and leading county family, whose farmstead at Wilmcote still survives (164). William was almost certainly educated at the local grammar school; and as a boy he probably saw performances by travelling players in the local guildhall. At about eighteen, he married Anne Hathaway of Shottery (165). He soon left Stratford for London, where he joined an acting company and became a playwright. His success was great, and with his wealth he bought New Place, one of the biggest houses in Stratford, to which he retired and died in 1616. His elder daughter Susanna lived nearby in Hall's Croft, whose rooms are still to be seen furnished in period style (page 51).

Our knowledge of the family in the Elizabethan age is derived from incidental references in contemporary sources. The practice of recording births, marriages and burials was by this time firmly established, so that reference to parish registers can establish the number, sex and age of individuals within family groups. Families were normally large, the rate of infant mortality was high and the expectation of life was much shorter than at present. Shakespeare himself died when he was 52. In Shakespeare's time much superstition still surrounded birth and christening ceremonies of a baby. There were traditional procedures and customs observed in betrothal and marriage, too. The upper classes believed that marriages should be profitable for parents, so that in this sense children were regarded as assets. Handbooks advised parents how to bestow their children in marriage, or summarized the relationship of man and wife, not to mention telling parents how to get their

children "to frame their gesture to a revered and dutiful behaviour towards others." Bringing up children varied according to the status of the family. Rich children were often left to the care of nursemaids and tutors, with only occasional parental intervention. Lower down the social scale the family lived and ate together (166). When an animal was killed, for example, the children would be sent to neighbours with gifts as a reminder that they should do the same when they had a killing (167). There were few changes and excitements in an average family home, though the advent of tobacco must have introduced novel social consequences (168). On the whole the children of the age were regarded as miniature adults and, as depicted in this painting of young King James I, they were dressed in exactly the same style of clothes as their elders (169). Play and games were not thought essential to a boy or a girl's development. Parental discipline was severe.

168

169

167

Education in Elizabethan England was good, and illiteracy was not too widespread, even among the poor. During Elizabeth's reign five schools were founded which became famous in later times: Repton (1559), Merchant Taylors (1561), Rugby (1567), Uppingham (1584), and Harrow (1590). Tudor England saw the foundation or refoundation of many grammar schools, both by the Crown, ecclesiastics, merchants and the landed gentry, the endowments often coming from the revenues of the lands once owned by the chantries and guilds. At least 360 grammar schools were in existence by 1575. Ashbourne School in Derbyshire was founded in 1585 by the Queen herself (170), while the Grammar school at Ashby de la Zouch, Leicestershire, established by Henry Hastings, third Earl of Huntingdon, in 1567, typified the country free schools which arose at this time. The grammar school at Stratford-upon-Avon—Shakespeare's school—was once the school of the town's medieval guild, re-

170

171

founded by Edward VI in 1553. At Stratford education was free for the sons of burgesses. No school registers exist, but there is no reason to doubt that Shakespeare, the son of one of Stratford's leading burgesses, was educated here (171). This was one of the best grammar schools in England. Entrants were expected to know their letters, learned with the help of a hornbook (173) and to write their names. Later, they received a classical education. Constant repetition, translation and examination "without the book" were the order of the day, and clearly the process of learning—with long schooldays and strict discipline—was expected to be long and irksome. Texts of classical authors, and standard Latin and French grammars were used, as well as books of writing examples (172). Handwriting, like that of the Queen herself, could be beautiful (174).

173

174

172

The ordinary countryman worked hard to grow food for his family and produce to sell (176). The servile conditions of land-holding had mostly given way to the payment of money rents. But the land was still largely cultivated on the old communal medieval system of open fields, with areas of commons, wastes and woodlands, alongside the lord's demesne farm or enclosures of more recent date. The succession of the seasons, with their uncertain weather, governed the routine of ploughing, sowing, reaping and harvesting (175). With his farming background Shakespeare's references to crops, gardens, horses and livestock, country characters, craftsmen and gardeners, give a vivid picture of village life. In the days when horses played such a vital role, the blacksmith provided an invaluable service (177). Crops consisted chiefly of red and white wheat, rye for bread-corn, barley and hops for malt-

175 176

177

ing, and oats. Various kinds of beans, pease and vetches were grown, while flax and hemp were local crops. The garden was soon regarded both as an investment and adornment. Cabbage and the sweet Spanish potato were known to Shakespeare and references to vineyards and vinefields are common. The flower garden became an adjunct to any house of standing. The formal knott garden, such as may still be seen at New Place, Stratford-upon-Avon, was a popular feature and led by a "pleached-bower" of crabtrees and honey-suckle to the kitchen garden and orchard. Several gardening handbooks were published at this time containing useful advice on pruning and other horticultural matters (178). John Gerarde's *The Herball* (1597) was a valuable reference work.

178

Since communications were hard and local communities mostly self-sufficing, sports and pastimes were traditional and handed down from medieval times. The right to hunt, whether chasing the deer or hawking with the falcon, had always been jealously guarded by the monarch and the great lords of the land (179). Shakespeare probably left Stratford as a young man for poaching deer in the park of Sir Thomas Lucy at Charlecote. True or not,

Shakespeare displays a remarkable knowledge of the chase. Elizabeth's palace of Nonsuch was the scene of frequent hunts (page 52) and she herself enjoyed the sport—as did James I— often taking a picnic lunch (180). In his famous hunting handbook, *The Noble Arte of Venerie* (1575), George Turbeville offered a complete guide, even down to the picnic menu: cold loin of veal, cold capon, beef, goose, pigeon pie, cold mutton, powdered neats'

179

180

181

tongues, gammon of bacon and "sausages and savoury knacks." Falconry was equally popular with the Queen (182) and James I (181). Though they might not participate in them the ordinary countrymen were naturally interested in these rural sports. For them the coursing of hares and rabbits was popular, as also cockfighting with its attendant gambling. Sometimes also groups of strolling players or itinerant ballad-mongers turned up in the small towns or country houses to present their entertainment. The appearance of the pedlar —the prototype of Shakespeare's Autolycus similarly provided a diversion in the remoter parts, as he offered for sale a miscellany of trinkets and "ribands of all the colours i' the rainbow" or "a bundle of new ballads", with tales recited "to a very doleful tune."

Alongside the sports already mentioned country folk found relaxation in watching and taking part in other amusements. Country dancing and maypole dancing on the village green were universally popular (183, 184). Holy-days, wakes, festivals of sheep shearing and harvesting, were marked by traditional celebrations. In *The Winter's Tale* Shakespeare recreates the atmosphere of a sheep-shearing feast, when the good dame dispensed hospi-tality to all comers and "would sing her song and dance her turn." Local games were held of tumbling, wrestling, fencing, riding, throwing the hammer and tossing the staff. A famous one—the Cotswold games—took place at Dover's Hill in the Cotswolds (185). It included coursing matches for greyhounds, running races, cudgel play, leaping, wrestling and throwing the sledge—with dancing, music, even of bagpipes, interspersed in the pro-

183

184

gramme. These games may appear rough and strenuous, but to people living in an age that loved bear-baiting, bull-baiting and cock-fighting the spectacle of physical suffering upset few. Even football as then played, commended by some as "conducive both to health and strength," was described by Philip Stubbes as "a friendly kind of fight . . . a bloody and murdering practice." Angling, bowls (186), quoit-throwing and skittles were criticized less, and fishing at any rate provided food (187). As to indoor recreations, children played games much like those which survive in country districts; and their elders enjoyed a number of forfeit games, dice and tables, and visits to the tavern. The ordinary man dis-liked the Puritan wish to repress his pleasure.

185

186 187

CHAPTER FIVE
ADVENTURE AND PROFIT

SHAKESPEARE lived in an age of acute competition and speculation. The merchant and rising middle class wanted above all to succeed and to acquire monetary wealth. Under their impulse new institutions fostered trade and raised capital for new ventures. A favourite practice of courtiers and their friends was to obtain patents from the Crown, conferring the exclusive rights to certain business ventures—frequently to the detriment of the common good.

Money conferred power, status and influence; in an age when public morality was low company promoters and speculators were not slow to embark on questionable transactions in the hope of making a fortune. The public service gave large scope for their activities, and State officials were not slow to exploit their positions to amass wealth. Sir George Carey, for example, made a private fortune as treasurer of the war in Ireland toward the end of Elizabeth's reign, by falsifying clothing and other accounts.

One of the most attractive fields of speculation was land. Apart from offering prospects of good investment, land ownership it could also gratify social ambition. In the hope of founding a county family many a successful merchant, official or lawyer would speculate in real estate, either by buying, selling, lending or even litigating. Given shrewdness and persistence a man like George Stoddart of London, a grocer, was able to transform himself into a land-owner of considerable wealth within a few years.

This land-hunger, accompanied by agrarian and economic changes arising from growing enclosure of common land for pasture, brought real hardship upon the peasantry, and considerable unrest throughout the country between 1558 and 1603. Philip Stubbes wrote in 1593 that enclosures were "the causes why rich men eat up poor men as beasts do eat grass . . . They take in and inclose commons, moors, heaths, and other common pastures, where-out the poor commonalty were wont to have all their forage and feeding for their cattle, and (which is more) corn for themselves to live upon." There were many similar complaints and in 1596 riots broke out in several districts, and again in the early years of James I's reign. A pamphlet of the time expressed the grievances of the peasants: "The world with us of the country runs upon the old rotten wheels. For all the northern cloth that is woven in our country will scarce make a gown to keep Charity warm: she goes so a-cold. Rich men never had more money, and Covetousness had never less pity. There was never in any age more money stirring, nor never yet more stir to get money. Farmers are now slaves to racking young prodigal landlords. These landlords are more servile slaves to their own riots and luxury."

High living and ostentatious rivalry characterized the class-conscious gentry or would-be gentry. For those with pretensions to advancement and money to spend, honours could usually be bought. Although Elizabeth conferred knighthoods sparingly James I sold titles on a big scale. In his first year as King he created 838 knights; in 1611 he instituted the rank of baronet—costing over £1,000—a hereditary knight who was to take precedence over all other knights except the Knights of the Garter. Officially the proceeds of this new creation were to go towards colonizing Ulster in Ireland, but few doubted that the money was used by James himself. No longer did a man gain his knighthood solely in battle; a new order of "carpet knight" had been established. In *Twelfth Night*, when Viola asks what sort of man her opponent in the dual is, Sir Toby Belch replies, "He is knight, dubb'd with unhatch'd rapier and on carpet consideration; but he is a devil in private brawl . . ." The uncle of the poet Robert Herrick, a goldsmith, was knighted for "making a Hole in a great diamond the King doth wear," and even a man who had married one of the Queen's laundresses was found to be a knight. That James I should also have elevated his favourite,

George Villiers, to a dukedom showed how far the medieval concept of nobility had been left behind.

The fact that Shakespeare's father had secured a grant of a coat-of-arms in 1596 further shows the workings of the social system at that time. His record of public service at Stratford-upon-Avon, for example as Bailiff, may well have deserved recognition, but his son William, the playwright, actor and theatre shareholder had already won success and fame in London and found favour at the Court. He also had money to spend on property and next year bought New Place, the best house in Stratford. Moreover, it should be remembered that as a glover and wool dealer John Shakespeare was typical of the rising commercial class who contributed so much to the nation's prosperity in Elizabeth's reign. It is interesting to note that it was the merchant class of subjects which Francis Bacon in his essay *Of Empire* singled out as providing the lifeblood of the national economy, and the source of enterprise: "If they flourish not, a kingdom may have good limbs, but they will have empty veins, and nourish little."

By 1600, English trade, especially in wool and cloth, was flourishing. Commercial speculation became fashionable at Court, and the gentry began to farm for profit. Merchant expansion took place against a background of inflation in Europe, worsened by the shipment of precious metals from the New World (188). This was an age notorious for its rising prices. The Queen's own financial difficulties were increased largely owing to the debased coinage which she inherited. Among the new coins issued during her reign was the three-farthing piece bearing the words, "A rose without a thorn" (195). As the country's economy expanded more coins were struck and circulated (193). Not until James I's reign did the first coin bearing the legend "Great Britain, France and Ireland" appear (194). Since Christopher Columbus had discovered America in 1492, Englishmen had taken the

lead in maritime enterprise. In Europe, too, the London-based Company of Merchant Adventurers had been seeking to develop the Baltic and Scandinavian markets (192). Under their guidance the first English voyage of exploration was undertaken in 1553 to search for a north-east passage to China through the Arctic seas, with a view to opening up trade centres in northern and eastern lands. The expedition achieved little, except the founding

of the Muscovy Company in 1555. This enterprise naturally produced a demand for ships and seamen skilled in navigation (188, 191). John Dee's *Arte of Navigation* published in 1577 suggests that the spirit of maritime expansion had permeated the life of the whole country (190).

192

194

195

Though rising in commercial importance, London had only the nave of St. Paul's Cathedral as a forum for transacting commerce. It fell to Sir Thomas Gresham to fill the gap in 1566 by building a bourse or Exchange (196, 197). In 1571 Queen Elizabeth commanded that it should be called the Royal Exchange. Fynes Moryson thought it "the most stately building in that kind that I have seen in Europe or Turkey." Hogenberg depicted a well-proportioned, solid stone building set around a paved quadrangle (198). The ground floor served as a meeting place for merchants, while the upper floor provided a shopping centre where traders could display their goods. Gresham's Exchange soon proved to be "a glorious bourse . . . for the meeting of merchants of all countries where any traffic is to be had." England's trade was being taken to the far corners of the world. Merchant

196 197

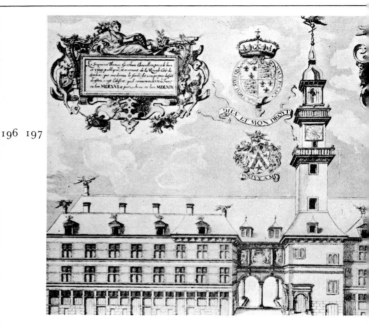

198

adventurers had long been exploring possible ways to the East, both overland through the Middle East and by sea around the Cape of Good Hope. They had founded another great institution of the merchant world, the East India Company (200). The initial capital was subscribed by a group of London merchants and financiers. The Queen gave official approval by granting a charter to the promoters in 1599. Next spring five ships set sail to launch the Company on its amazing career as "the pioneer of imperial England in the East" (page 53). Apart from the political role the Company later came to assume in India, the commercial benefit to England was immeasurable. Many treasures from the East came into the possession of English families, such as this Ming porcelain cup (199).

199

200

THE OLD EAST INDIA HOUSE, LEADENHALL ST.

From a copy of a Drawing by Virtue in the possession of Robt. Graves, Esq., A.R.A.

Next to wool, cloth-making was a great industry in Elizabethan England and flourished not only in urban centres but in the cottages of rural workers throughout the country (201). Supplies of wool came from the local market, which also provided the outlet for the finished product. The wool and cloth trade encouraged ancillary trades, such as dyeing, tailoring (202), glove-making, thread-making, and hat-making (203). Sartorial tastes, especially of the upper classes, encouraged the manufacture of lace, silk weaving and other luxury products, and the influx of Protestant refugees from the Netherlands gave an impetus to these new, as well as to some of the older, crafts. Apothecaries and barbers catered for the more pressing needs of those in pain or in need of a haircut (204, 205). In London, particularly, groups of skilled craftsmen met the domestic needs of the court ladies

201

202

203

204

and noblemen; the goldsmiths became important not only for making objects of great beauty and value, but also for acting as bankers (206). Swords, knives and daggers were still in great demand, as also mousetraps, candlesticks, lanterns, bird cages and other fancy goods handled by the milliners and haberdashers. The making of armour, now worn more for decoration than protection, continued to be a serious and lucrative business. Splendid examples of the armourer's craft have survived, for instance in the beautiful suit of armour made for the young Charles I preserved in the Tower of London. Spurs, too, continued to have a practical use (207), while leather provided material for jerkins, purses, dagger sheaths and footwear (208).

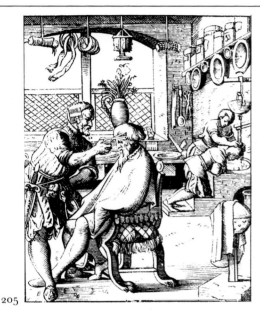

205

206

207

208

The Lord Chancellor's seat in the House of Lords, a large woolsack (page 54) was adopted in Edward III's reign as a reminder of the importance of the wool trade to the country. English sheep and wool were reputed to be the best in the world. Evidence of the prosperity brought by sheep rearing and cloth weaving survives in the fine churches built by the wool merchants, for example in the Cotswolds and in Suffolk, which reflect the prosperity of the loom (209). The shepherd was idealized by Elizabethan writers (211). The boom in the wool trade, however, brought problems, particularly arising from the enclosure of common lands to make way for sheep. To help the wool trade the Queen decreed that "all persons above the age of six years" should wear, with few exceptions, the city flat cap (210). Other minor industries developed, for example the tin and copper mines of Cornwall (215), the

209   210

212

211

extraction of china clay for pottery (213), the northern coal industry, and metal manufactures in the Midlands. One of England's richest natural resources was timber, essential for building, ship-building, and carpentry (212). The Forest of Arden reached the outskirts of Stratford-upon-Avon and provided the oak and elm used in the half-timbered buildings of the town over many centuries. But the expansion of iron-ore smelting in Elizabethan times put timber in short supply. Although Government censorship handicapped book production, Fleet Street was already the home of printing presses. Printers satisfied the growing thirst for knowledge. Some of these books, such as Holinshed's *Chronicle*, provided Shakespeare with his source material. Printing also created a demand for paper (214) and made possible the issue of broadsheets and, later, newspapers.

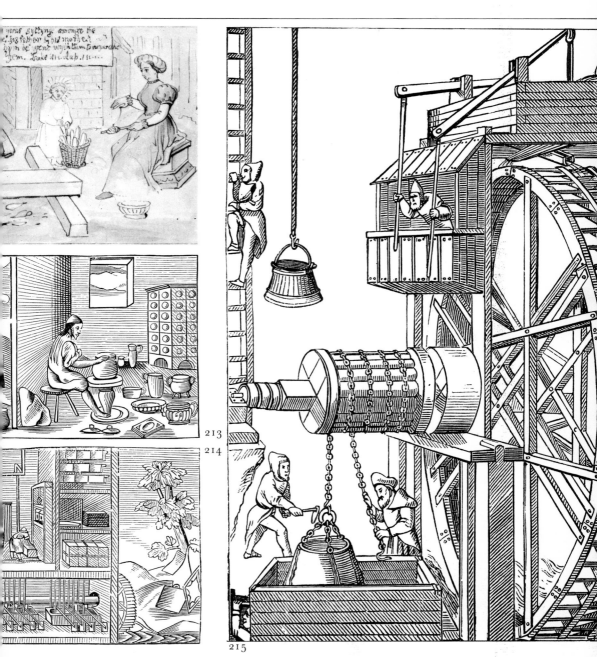

213
214

CHAPTER SIX

WIDENING HORIZONS

TO THOSE who have seen television pictures of moon landings it is hard to realize that in Shakespeare's day, news and opinions could not be rapidly disseminated. Reports of discoveries, wars, and events overseas, took weeks and months to reach London and when passed orally from one to another often became distorted. As a result people tended to be more excitable and emotional than they are today. When Shakespeare talked of "rumour, painted full of tongues" he knew from experience that wild gossip and alarm all too often produced unnecessary panic, for instance at the time of the false report of a Spanish invasion in 1599.

Apart from the official records it is to the writers of the period that the historian must turn for information about the events and happenings of the period, especially those relating to the discoveries of the explorers and seamen adventurers. Richard Eden's *History of Travayle* (1577) has much to say of the Portuguese and Spaniards, who between them had proved "no land uninhabitable nor sea unnavigable." Following the equator, they had explored both the eastern and western hemispheres, finding human beings or calm seas from end to end. Emphasis is given to the greatness of the English adventurers and their exploits by Richard Hakluyt in his *Principal Navigations* (1589). This work narrated the adventures of sailors who had taken part in perilous exploits in unknown seas and in a much enlarged version was re-published by

Samuel Purchas in 1625 as *Hakluytus Posthumus, or Purchas his Pilgrimes*. It has with some justice been described as a "great prose epic of the English nation."

Certainly the half-century of Shakespeare's life saw momentous happenings in exploration and colonization. To mention only a few: Manila, Philippine Islands, was founded by the Spanish; Russia and Persia were discovered from the north by Anthony Jenkinson; Martin Frobisher sailed in search of the northwest passage; Englishmen led raids to West Africa and the West Indies; Sir Francis Drake circumnavigated the world; Dutch sailors explored the Dutch East Indies guided by English pilots; Sir Humphrey Gilbert took possession of Newfoundland in the name of Queen Elizabeth; Sir Walter Raleigh claimed Virginia for the Queen; Virginia Dare became the first white child born in America; the Marquis de la Roche obtained from Henry IV of France a commission to conquer Canada; Samuel de Champlain sailed up the St. Lawrence River and brought a colony to settle and found Quebec; Port Royal was founded in Nova Scotia by the French; and a settlement was established in the Bermudas.

Most of these epoch-making discoveries took place, it should be remembered, at a time when much of Europe was ravaged by war. England, too, was threatened— first by political and religious problems within, and then by the threat of invasion from without. The urge to explore was motivated by the desire to attack the Spaniards at every possible point and at the same time to discover new sources of wealth and trade for the Queen and her subjects. Only later did the idea of planting colonies as permanent outposts of English trade and life suggest itself and it was not until after Elizabeth's death that the various projects of English colonization began to take practical effect.

Shakespeare seems to have kept very well in touch with current affairs. Scattered throughout his plays are topical references, some of which are readily recognizable, others of which still defy explanation. There are also passages which reflect the mood of the times, and as such should form part of any commentary on outlook and manners. A few examples must suffice. Shakespeare's reference in *Love's Labour's Lost* to "frozen Muscovits," "sea-sick from Muscovy," was prompted by the frequent English embassies to Moscow, and the visits of Russians to London by the Arctic northern route. In *Macbeth* his witches sang, "Her husband's to Aleppo gone, master of the Tiger"— a reference to the ship *Tiger* of London which used to visit Tripoli (the port of Aleppo) in Syria and Alexandria in Egypt. Shakespeare's allusions to the discovery of faraway islands are also topical, as for

instance, in *The Tempest*, set in the "still-vexed Bermoothes." A storm off the Bermudas had in fact wrecked an English company during a voyage to Virginia in 1609. It is not known whether Shakespeare himself ever visited Europe but several times he pokes fun and ridicules those who had been abroad for being "antic, affecting, fantasticoes, tuners of new accents."

It is against this background that the scientific advances of the age are to be seen. The centuries of the Middle Ages had seen little advance in man's knowledge of the universe, physical sciences, and the human body with its ailments and cures. From the discovery of new lands arose a new questioning spirit of scientific enquiry and experiment. This resulted in great advances in astronomy and its uses, and ultimately enabled physics to emerge from alchemy, and medicine out of witchcraft and old wives' tales. This was doubtless due to the enthusiasm and skill of a few. The achievement is perhaps all the more surprising because while the Court, the wealthier citizens of London, and some noblemen were patrons of the arts, few supported scientific research. Nor did Parliament itself contribute much to the process.

Without ports and ships, neither the security nor the commerce of the island kingdom could be guaranteed. The pre-eminence of London as a commercial port has already been emphasized (216). Outside London, Bristol already had behind it a tradition of service to overseas trade and seafaring adventure. During the Middle Ages, much of the cloth and wool from the prosperous city of Coventry and the Cotswolds had found an export outlet through this port. In 1497, John Cabot set out from Bristol to reach Cape Breton Island in fifty-two days, and it was from this port that he later sailed to Greenland and Labrador. Smith's plan of Bristol surveyed in 1568 confirms its importance by this time (217). In-

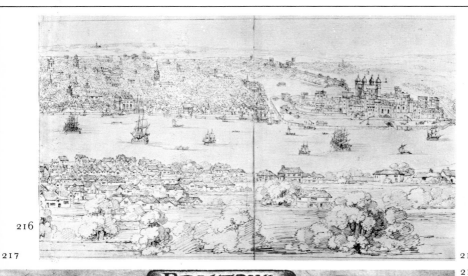

216

218

217

BRISTOW.

measured & laid in
Platforme, by me
W. Smith, at my
being at Bristow,
the 30. & 31. July.
An°. Dm°. 1568.

Redcliff.

219

creasingly it was to become the chief gateway to the west. The Channel ports also played their part, though more from a naval than a commercial point of view. Chief among these were Plymouth, Portsmouth, Dover and Chatham. Rochester was also an important naval base apart from being a great medieval centre of church and government conveniently situated between Canterbury and London (219). Except for size, men-of-war and merchant ships differed little in appearance, equipment, or performance. As compared with the huge Spanish galleons, the ships built by the English were smaller and faster and much more capable of withstanding the rough weather of the open Atlantic (218, 220).

220

The Elizabethan navy comprised three sorts of vessels, of which "the one serveth for the wars, the other for burden, and the third for fishermen . . . Certes there is no prince in Europe that hath a more beautiful or gallant sort of ships than the Queen's majesty of England at this present." This superiority of the English ship was in Harrison's opinion due to its unique design: "For strength, assurance, nimbleness, and swiftness of sailing, there are no vessels in the world to be compared with ours." The pioneering demand for fine sailing craft inspired first class ship-building in Elizabeth's reign. Under her Stuart successors the controversial levy of ship money gave extra revenue for ship-building, which allowed the

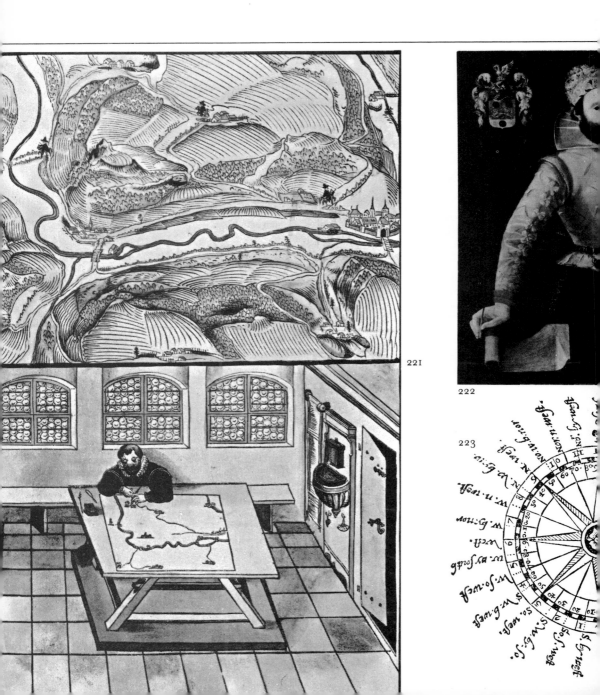

221

222

223

building of *The Sovereign of the Seas* by Phineas Pett (222) in 1637—the largest ship afloat. The urge to explore also led to the making of maps (221) of lands from Russia (224) to Florida (225). The sea and its mysterious horizons became subjects of serious study and speculation. Charts, navigational aids, and books on navigation and pilotage became numerous.

The practical treatise of Martin Cortes on the *Sphere and the Art of Navigation*, translated by Richard Eden in 1561, was very popular. William Bourne's *Regiment of the Sea* (1573) was designed to supplement it, while *Seaman's Secrets*, published by John Davis in 1594, offered guidance to mariners wishing to proceed to any point of the compass (223).

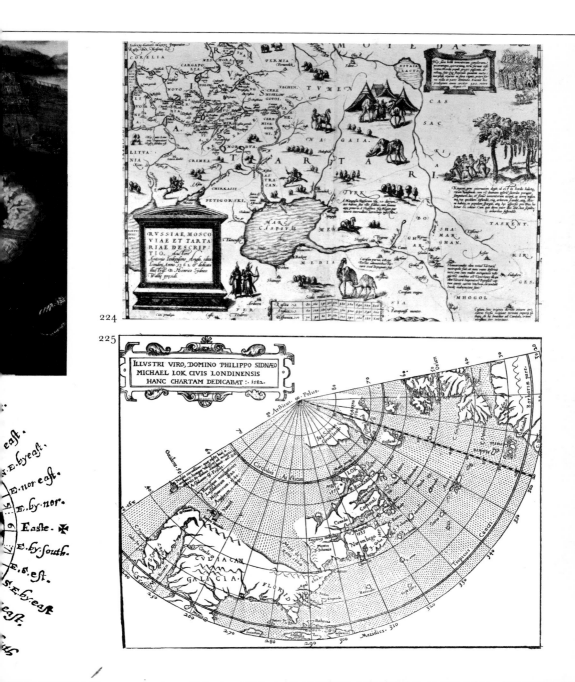

224

225

To boys of Shakespeare's age the discovery of the New World was as fascinating as the American space trips to the moon in our time. Richard Hakluyt echoed the pride of his contemporaries: the English nation has "excelled all the nations and peoples of the earth . . . in searching the most opposite corners and quarters of the world, and . . . in compassing the vast globe of the earth more than once." The two outstanding seamen of the day were Sir John Hawkins of Plymouth (228) and his Devonshire cousin Sir Francis Drake (226). They first sailed together on slave-trading expeditions to the Spanish Main in 1566 and 1567. Later, Drake made three voyages to the West Indies to capture Spanish treasure and strike a blow on behalf of Protestantism against Catholic Spain. In 1577 he embarked upon his famous three-year voyage in the *Golden Hind* (227). Rounding the tip of South

226   227

228   229

America through the treacherous Magellan Straits he crossed the Pacific and Indian Oceans, and sailed back to Plymouth by way of South Africa. Drake was knighted by the Queen's command in 1581, the year in which he acquired Buckland Abbey as his home (229). The *Golden Hind* was probably very similar to the one depicted by Breugel (230) and the ships painted on the lid of what is traditionally regarded as Drake's chest (page 55). In a similar manner Sir John Hawkins, a bold and skilful navigator, led a series of raids on the Spanish colonies. Hawkins was a many-sided man: Treasurer of the Navy, merchant and ship-owner, seaman and naval administrator, designer of ships, strategist, politician, and diplomat.

In 1574 Sir Humphrey Gilbert had presented a plan to Queen Elizabeth to find a southern route to the Pacific. In 1578 he obtained a patent to "plant" America—to settle a community and to provide for its government and needs. Unfortunately the expedition which he led to Newfoundland for this purpose five years later failed. It fell to Walter Raleigh, Gilbert's half-cousin, to fulfil his dream of colonizing the American mainland. Raleigh obtained a similar patent in 1584. In 1585 Raleigh sent out an expedition under Sir Richard Grenville (231)—immortalised by his fight in the *Revenge* in 1591—to establish the first English colony of Virginia on Roanoak Island. Initially over a hundred settlers were planted (232). But when Grenville returned with supplies for them the following year he found that the entire colony, threatened by starvation and the hostility of the Indians, had returned to England with

231

232

233

Drake who had called at the settlement on his way back from the West Indies. Thus in 1587 Raleigh launched a second attempt to plant a colony in Virginia under John White but the whole community had disappeared when ships arrived from England bringing supplies. The planting of settlers in a virgin country without adequate preparations and established lines of communication was clearly a hazardous business and it was not until 1607 that Virginia was re-founded. Among the settlers was Captain John Smith, who became head of the colony in 1608 (234). Smith is said to have been rescued when taken a prisoner by the Indians by the Indian Princess Pocahontas. Smith's *Generall Historie of Virginia* (1624) is a rich source of information on this earliest chapter of English colonisation. Picture (233) is a plate from the book.

234

The Tudor period saw a revolution in physical science throughout Europe. Before, most people believed that the earth was the fixed centre of the universe, over which God presided (235). Copernicus propounded an entirely new Solar system of astronomy in 1543, wherein all the planets revolved about the sun. His ideas quickly attracted support from England. The Danish astronomer Tycho Brahe produced an important work on comets (237). The English scholars apparently used instruments in their observations, particularly "perspective glasses," which may have anticipated Galileo's telescope of 1609. All these discoveries helped the plotting of courses, the drawing of accurate maps, and the making of more refined instruments (236, 238). As astronomy grew, astrology declined, and

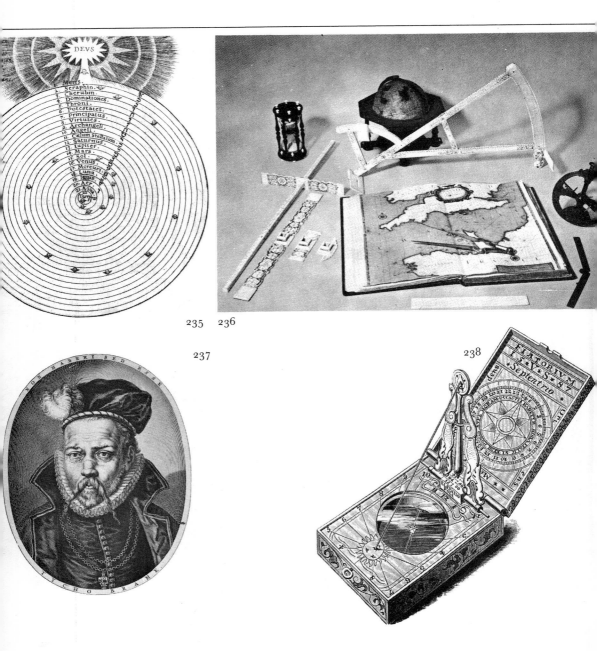

235   236

237

238

fortune-tellers were suspected for relying on tricks. Though modern chemistry was unknown, medieval alchemy was widely practised (239). Students tried to turn base metal into gold (240), and to seek the elixir of life—the correct proportion of the elements in the human body. Inevitably, it was the hope of producing gold from base metals that gave alchemy its popularity, and attracted royal support. In 1565, the Queen accepted the offer of one Cornelius Alvetanus to produce for her 50,000 marks of pure gold annually, and gave him rooms in Somerset House. Unfortunately his experiments, like those of others (241), ended in failure and he was imprisoned in the Tower.

240

241

Medicine was in its infancy in Tudor times. Though research on the Continent was already producing new ideas about the human anatomy and medical science in general; to a large extent the treatment of the sick in England at this time was still based on the writings of the second-century Greek physician, Galen. Surgery was unbelievably clumsy and hazardous; anaesthetics had not yet been discovered. Certainly a signboard of 1623 (page 56) showing a practitioner drawing teeth, amputating a leg, bleeding and treating a tumour, does not inspire confidence, any more than the amputation saw itself used at that time (243). Drugs were sold by apothecaries, who operated apparently without supervision. Yet this was a time of change and experiment. Medical professorships had been founded at Oxford and Cambridge by Henry VIII and the College of Physicians and the Company of Barber-Surgeons was already founded before Elizabeth came to the throne. Anatomical research

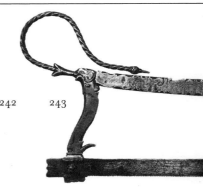

242   243

244

Select Observations

ON

ENGLISH

BODIES:

OR,

Cures both Empericall and Historicall, performed upon very eminent Persons in desperate Diseases.

First, written in Latine by Mr. *John Hall* Physician, living at *Stratford* upon *Avon* in *Warwick-shire*, where he was very famous, as also in the Counties adjacent, as appeares by these Observations drawn out of severall hundreds of his, as choysest.

was encouraged and the Queen gave permission in 1565 for the College of Physicians to carry out human dissections. Well known surgeons of the day were John Gale, William Clowes and John Woodall, while among physicians William Harvey, the son of a Kentish yeoman, distinguished himself by discovering the circulation of the blood. A prominent provincial doctor was John Hall, Shakespeare's son-in-law, who lived at Stratford-upon-Avon. A selection from Hall's private casebook was published for students in 1657, entitled *Select Observations on English Bodies* (242). Hall's eminence as a doctor was recognized by his colleagues. His remedies were original and frequently drastic, but based largely on herbs, purges and poultices. His house, Hall's Croft, a fine Elizabethan house complete with dispensary, still survives today at Stratford-upon-Avon, a living reminder of perhaps the greatest period of English social history (244, 245).

245

FURTHER READING

J. B. Black, *The Reign of Elizabeth* (Oxford University Press, London and New York, 1936)

Ivor Brown, *Shakespeare and his World* (Lutterworth Press, London, 1964; H. Z. Walck Inc., New York, 1964)

M. St. Claire Byrne, *Elizabethan Life in Town and Country* (Methuen, London, 1925; revised edition, 1961; Barnes & Noble, New York, 1962)

Levi Fox, *The Borough Town of Stratford-upon-Avon* (The Corporation of Stratford-upon-Avon, 1951)

Martin Holmes, *Elizabethan London* (Cassell, London, 1971; Frederick A. Praeger, New York, 1971)

Maurice Hussey, *The World of Shakespeare and his Contemporaries* (Heinemann, London, 1971)

J. E. Neale, *Queen Elizabeth I* (Jonathan Cape, London, 1934; St. Martin's Press, New York, 1959)

Allardyce Nicoll, *The Elizabethans* (Cambridge University Press, London, 1957)

Allardyce Nicoll (ed.), *Shakespeare in His own Age—Shakespeare Survey 17* (Cambridge University Press, London, 1964)

Lu Emily Pearson, *Elizabethans at Home* (Oxford University Press, London, 1957; Stanford University Press, Calif., 1957)

A. L. Rowse, *The England of Elizabeth* (Macmillan, London, 1950; Crowell, Collier & Macmillan, New York, 1969)

L. F. Salzman, *England in Tudor Times* (Batsford, London, 1926; Russell & Russell, New York, 1969)

Shakespeare's England (2 vols.) (Oxford University Press, London and New York, 1916)

John Dover Wilson, *Life in Shakespeare's England* (Cambridge University Press, London, 1911; re-issued by Penguin, London, 1968; Barnes & Noble, New York, 1968)

Louis B. Wright, *Middle-Class Culture in Elizabethan England* (University of North Carolina Press, 1935; reprinted by Cornell University Press, Ithaca, N.Y., 1958; Methuen, London, 1959)

PICTURE CREDITS

INDEX